FINISHING BASICS

Sam Allen

 Sterling Publishing Co., Inc.   New York

INCHES TO CENTIMETERS

INCHES	CM	INCHES	CM	INCHES	CM	INCHES	CM
1/8	0.3	9	22.9	24	61.0	39	99.1
1/4	0.6	10	25.4	25	63.5	40	101.6
3/8	1.0	11	27.9	26	66.0	41	104.1
1/2	1.3	12	30.5	27	68.6	42	106.7
5/8	1.6	13	33.0	28	71.1	43	109.2
3/4	1.9	14	35.6	29	73.7	44	111.8
7/8	2.2	15	38.1	30	76.2	45	114.3
1	2.5	16	40.6	31	78.7	46	116.8
2	5.1	17	43.2	32	81.3	47	119.4
3	7.6	18	45.7	33	83.8	48	121.9
4	10.2	19	48.3	34	86.4	49	124.5
5	12.7	20	50.8	35	88.9	50	127.0
6	15.2	21	53.3	36	91.4		
7	17.8	22	55.9	37	94.0		
8	20.3	23	58.4	38	96.5		

Library of Congress Cataloging-in-Publication Data

Allen, Sam.
 Finishing basics / Sam Allen.
    p.   cm.
 Includes index.
 ISBN 0-8069-7228-9
 1. Wood finishing. I. Title.
TT325.A44 1992
684'.084—dc20

                                        91-21004
                                        CIP

10 9 8 7 6 5 4 3 2

Published in 1992 by Sterling Publishing Company, Inc.
387 Park Avenue South, New York, N.Y. 10016
© 1992 by Sam Allen
Distributed in Canada by Sterling Publishing
% Canadian Manda Group, P.O. Box 920, Station U
Toronto, Ontario, Canada M8Z 5P9
Distributed in Great Britain and Europe by Cassell PLC
Villiers House, 41/47 Strand, London WC2N 5JE, England
Distributed in Australia by Capricorn Link Ltd.
P.O. Box 665, Lane Cove, NSW 2066
Manufactured in the United States of America
All rights reserved

Sterling ISBN 0-8069-7228-9

Contents

INTRODUCTION

Wood finishing is one of the most popular areas of amateur woodworking. Whether you want to finish a project that you have built or a piece of unfinished furniture, or refinish an old piece, this book will guide you through the basics. (See Illus. i-1.) In the following pages, you will learn how to apply one of the most beautiful and versatile finishes, the hand-rubbed oil finish, and will soon be able to produce quality finishes that rival professionally applied finishes in appearance and durability.

This book is written for someone with little or no wood-finishing experience. The products and procedures described and illustrated have been chosen with the novice in mind. They are meant to be used for finishing or refinishing furniture, woodwork projects, and interior house woodwork such as built-in cabinets and doors. Large projects like house painting and exterior staining are beyond the scope of this book. If you are interested in more information on advanced techniques and products, consult my book *Wood Finisher's Handbook*.

Environmental and health concerns about the solvents traditionally used in finishing products have motivated the finishing-products industry to develop a number of new products that are safer and easier to use than older ones. Because most of these new products are water-based, different techniques are used to apply them. These new water-based products have been emphasized in this book, so even if you are an experienced wood finisher, much valuable information can be found in the following chapters.

Before you can finish a piece of wood properly, you have to know the properties of the particular species of wood you are working on. Therefore, Chapter 1 defines the properties of wood that affect finishing. It also contains a description of some of the more popular woods used for cabi-

Illus. i-1. In the following pages, you will learn the basics of finishing and refinishing furniture and cabinetry.

nets and ways to finish them. At this stage, it will probably be helpful if you refer to the Glossary on pages 123-126. This Glossary clarifies terms that appear throughout the book. Chapter 2 covers the tools and supplies that will be used to apply the finishing techniques described in this book.

A truly fine finish begins in the early stages of a project, with wood preparation. If the wood is not prepared properly, a smooth finish is impossible. Chapter 3 clarifies wood preparation.

The best finish to use on your first wood-finishing project is a hand-rubbed oil finish. Chapter 4 gives directions for applying such a finish. Though a rubbed oil finish is easy to apply and produces beautiful results, it is not suited to every project. The remaining chapters cover other types of finish that can be used when a rubbed oil finish is not appropriate. Chapter 5 covers the subject of stains and fillers. Chapter 6 gives directions for applying varnish. Other top coats are described in Chapter 7.

Steel wool and rubbing compounds can be used to smooth the surface of a varnish or lacquer top coat. Their use is described in Chapter 8. For some projects, paint is a more appropriate finish. Chapter 9 covers pertinent information about paint. And if the piece you are finishing is an antique reproduction or a "country"-style piece, you may want to apply an antique finish by following the directions in Chapter 10.

Pastel and pickled finishes use stains that have a great deal of white pigment. They can give a project a light, cheerful look or make it look like an antique that had an original coat of paint that has since worn off. You will learn several methods for applying pastel and pickled finishes in Chapter 11. If you want to refinish a piece of furniture, refer to Chapter 12. It describes how to strip off an old finish and apply a new one.

Whenever you use a product or technique you are unfamiliar with, practise on a piece of scrap wood. That way, you can determine if you like the finish before applying it to the actual project. You will also gain experience that will help you avoid problems with the application.

—Sam Allen

Chapter 1

PROPERTIES OF WOOD THAT AFFECT FINISHING

Wood is a complex material composed of fibres made of tiny cells. The type of wood and the way it is cut from the log both determine how the wood will accept a finish, and what it will look like when you are done.

If you were to look at the end of a log, you would see a cross-section of its cells. (See Illus.

1-1.) The familiar pattern of growth rings is formed by the annual growth pattern of the tree. In the middle of the log, you would see a small, dark spot. This is called the *pith*. It is a remnant of when the tree first started growing as a sapling.

As a tree grows, new cells are formed in a layer

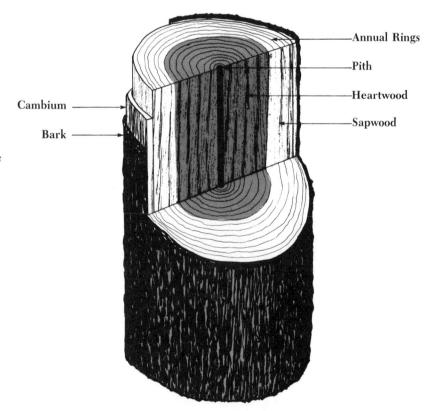

Illus. 1-1. This cutaway drawing of a log is labelled with the names of its various parts. Note how the tree rings appear in the log. When the log is cut into boards, the grain pattern will be formed by the parts of rings visible on the surface of the board.

Annual Rings

Pith

Heartwood

Sapwood

Cambium

Bark

just below the bark. This layer is called the *cambium*. When there is plenty of water available, growth is fast and the cells produced are large. The wood produced is called *spring* or *early* wood. When there is less water available, the cells are produced more slowly and they are small and dense. This wood is called *summer* or *late* wood. The visible tree rings are formed because of this growth pattern. In the spring, when there is a lot of moisture, the tree grows rapidly, producing large, soft cells. When summer comes and there is less moisture, the tree growth slows down and smaller, harder cells are made. In wet years wide rings are produced; in drought years, very small rings are produced.

Grain Pattern

The grain pattern on the face of a board is a result of how the saw cuts through the annual rings of the log. Boards can be cut from a log in several ways. The most common methods produce plain-sawn and quarter-sawn lumber (See Illus. 1-2.)

Plain-sawn lumber is the type of lumber you are probably most familiar with. The grain pattern on the face of a board is a series of long U shapes called a flat grain. Plain-sawn lumber is cut with the saw blade almost tangent to the annual rings of the tree. The rings show up on the

face of the board as elongated arcs because they are cut at a slight angle, due to the taper of the tree trunk.

Quarter-sawn lumber is cut differently. The saw blade is closer to a right angle with the rings. This means that the rings appear on the face of the board as a series of closely spaced parallel lines. The grain pattern of quarter-sawn lumber is called vertical grain. Some species of wood have *rays*. Rays are grain features that appear as small dark lines on the face of a board that is plain-sawn lumber, and as prominent irregular lines on the face of a board that is quarter-sawn lumber. Oak is a good example of a wood species that has prominent rays. (See Illus. 1-3.)

The grain patterns affect the finish in several ways. The most obvious effect is how the finish looks. Plain-sawn lumber will show a large variation in color, because the spring wood will absorb a stain more readily than the summer wood. (See Illus. 1-4.) Plain-sawing exposes wider bands of spring and summer wood. Quarter-sawn lumber will look fairly uniform, because the exposed bands of spring and summer wood are narrow and closely spaced. (See Illus. 1-5.)

Another difference between plain-sawn and quarter-sawn lumber is the way the finish adheres to the surface of the board. Quarter-sawn lumber gives the finish a better surface to stick

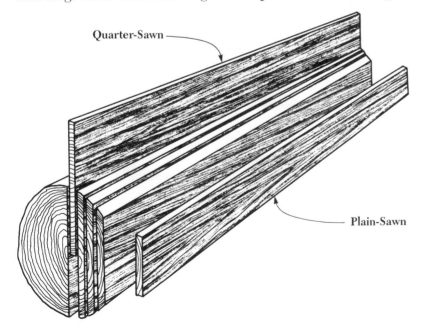

Quarter-Sawn

Plain-Sawn

Illus. 1-2. If you cut a log as shown in this illustration, the boards near the outside would be plain-sawn and the boards near the middle would be quarter-sawn. In actual practice, the log can be reoriented during the cutting to maximize the amount of either type of board.

Illus. 1-3. This quarter-sawn oak displays a prominent pattern of rays.

Illus. 1-5. Quarter-sawn lumber absorbs stain more evenly, making the grain pattern less prominent.

Illus. 1-4. Plain-sawn lumber shows a large variation in color when stained, because of the difference in the amount of stain absorbed by the spring and summer woods.

to, so the finish will be more durable. This characteristic isn't particularly important for interior projects, so the first priority in choosing a finish for such a project is how you want the finish to look. The finish on exterior projects will last much longer if it is applied to quarter-sawn lumber. That is the reason most wood siding has vertical grain.

Wood Color

The life processes of the tree take place in a narrow band below the bark; this band is called *sapwood*. Sapwood is usually light in color.

The wood closer to the center is called heartwood. In some trees, the heartwood is a dark color. This is due to chemicals and trace minerals that accumulate in the heartwood.

Each species of tree has a characteristic color of heartwood. There will be variations in color between boards due to different growing conditions. The heartwood of walnut is a rich brown color. Birch has a light reddish brown heart-wood, and oak has a medium reddish tan color.

The color of the wood plays an important role in how the project is finished. If you want to *enhance* the original color of the wood, apply a clear penetrating finish. If you want to *change* the color, you must use a stain. Sometimes you want the same color as the wood, but you need to even out variations in color between boards. In this case, apply a stain that matches the color of the board, and adjust the color intensity of each board by varying the amount of stain you wipe off the board.

Pores

All trees have fluid vessels that transfer the sap from one part of the tree to another. Water and nutrients travel up from the roots to the leaves. In the leaves, sunlight reacts with the nutrients to make food for the tree. This food must then be distributed from the leaves throughout the tree.

When the tree is cut into lumber, these fluid vessels are exposed on the surface of the board. When they show on the face of the board, they are called pores. The size and pattern of the pores depends on the species of the tree. When the pores are large and easily visible, the wood is called *open-grained*. When the pores are small and not noticeable, the wood is called *closed-grained*. Oak is a good example of an open-grained wood. (See Illus. 1-21 on page 17.) Maple is a closed-grained wood. (See Illus. 1-20 on page 17.)

The way the pores are distributed also varies from one type of wood to another. Woods such as oak, ash, and elm are called *ring-porous*. The pores of ring-porous woods are concentrated in the spring wood. This means that the pore pattern follows the grain pattern. Finishing products such as stain will accumulate in the pores. This will accentuate the grain pattern of a ring-porous wood. You can highlight the grain pattern of a ring-porous wood by using a pigment-rich stain that will accumulate in the pores.

Black walnut is a semi–ring-porous wood. (See Illus. 1-27 on page 19.) The pores are larger and more concentrated in the spring wood, but there still are pores visible in the summer wood. This tends to make the board stain a more even color, but the pore pattern still accentuates the grain pattern.

A diffuse-porous wood has pores evenly distributed throughout the ring. In this case, the pores won't follow the grain pattern. If the pores are small, the wood is closed-grained and the pores don't have much effect on the finish. Birch is an example of a closed-grained, diffuse-porous wood. (See Illus. 1-14.) When an open-grained wood is diffuse-porous, the pores will tend to hide the grain pattern if you let the stain accumulate in them. Philippine mahogany is an example of an open-grained, diffuse-porous wood. (See Illus. 1-19.) You can diminish the effect of the pores by filling them.

When you finish an open-grained wood, you have to decide whether to fill the grain or leave it open. If you want a smooth, glossy surface, you must fill the grain. If you want the natural texture of the wood to show, use a finish that won't fill the grain. Filling the grain with a filler close to the color of the rest of the wood will hide the pore pattern. Using a filler that is lighter or darker than the rest of the wood will accentuate the pore pattern.

Knots

As a tree grows, branches grow out of the main trunk. A knot is the place where the branch is attached to the main trunk. In plain-sawn lumber, the knot usually shows up as a circle. In quarter-sawn lumber, the knot may show up as a long spike. (See Illus. 1-6.)

Knots will usually stain darker than the surrounding wood, making them a prominent visual aspect of the board. In some cases, knots are considered a decorative feature. (See Illus. 1-7.) In other cases, they are considered a defect. If you plan on using knots as decorative elements in a project, make sure they are tight knots. A tight knot is one that is intergrown with the rest of the board so that it cannot fall out. A loose knot is

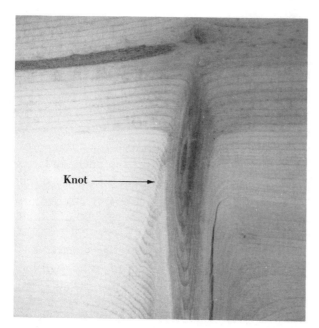

Illus. 1-6. Spike-like knots usually occur in quarter-sawn lumber.

Illus. 1-7. Tight knots can be used for decorative effect, as shown here on this panel door.

surrounded by a layer of bark. This occurs when the tree grows around a dead limb. A loose knot will eventually fall out, leaving a large hole in the board. Some knots contain a resin that can seep through paint and stain the surface, so special precautions must be taken when painting over knots.

Dimensional Change

The living cells of a tree are filled with fluid. When the tree is cut, the wood dries out. This causes the wood to shrink. When the log is cut into lumber, the boards are dried to a point where most of the moisture is gone and most of the shrinkage has taken place. The wood, however, will still be sensitive to moisture. Wood will absorb humidity from the air when the weather is wet, and swell. When the air is dry, the wood will shrink. (See Illus. 1-8.)

One of the main reasons for applying a finish to wood is to protect it from moisture. But all finishes will allow some humidity to get through. Therefore, the finish has to be flexible enough to "stretch" as the wood swells and shrinks. If the wood changes faster than the finish can handle, cracks will develop in the finish. One function of a finish is to slow down the rate that humidity is absorbed by the wood; this eliminates rapid dimensional change and allows the finish time to react to the gradual changes that will take place.

A finish must allow some humidity in and out of the board; this is called breathing. If the finish doesn't breathe, moisture can't get out of the board and becomes trapped below the surface of the finish. This can lead to blisters and peeling.

Hardwoods and Softwoods

The terms hardwood and softwood are used often in a woodworker's vocabulary. They don't indi-

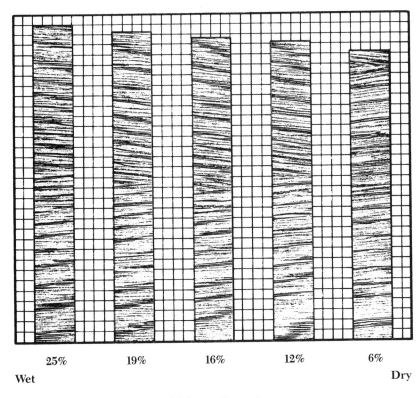

| 25% | 19% | 16% | 12% | 6% |

Wet   **Dry**

Moisture Content

Illus. 1-8. This graph shows how changes in moisture content can cause a board to shrink or swell. Wood will absorb moisture from the air, causing dimensional change to occur as the air humidity varies.

cate the actual hardness of the wood; rather, they describe the type of tree that produces the wood. Hardwoods come from trees that have broad leaves. (See Illus. 1-9.) Softwoods come from trees that have needles. (See Illus. 1-10.) Generally, softwoods have a softer surface than hardwoods, but there are some exceptions.

There is a big difference between softwoods and hardwoods when it comes to finishing. Softwoods such as pine and fir absorb a stain unevenly. This can lead to a blotchy or muddy appearance. Hardwoods usually absorb a stain evenly. Special procedures are needed when staining softwoods, if you want to achieve a uniform look.

Density

A wood's hardness can be measured by its density. Wood density is expressed as the ratio of the weight of the wood to an equal volume of water. If the density is less than one, then the wood will float in water. A wood with a high density will be

Illus. 1-9. Lumber that is cut from trees with broad leaves is called hardwood.

Illus. 1-10. *Lumber that comes from needle-bearing trees is called softwood.*

hard and durable. Woods with low density are soft and flexible. (See Illus. 1-11.)

Density plays a role in wood finishing because a dense wood won't absorb as much finish as a softer wood. Also, since a dense wood will have a harder surface, it is not as important that you choose a hard protective coating for the wood. For example, a walnut tabletop could be given a durable penetrating oil finish. A pine tabletop will dent and scratch easily, so if you want to protect it you might need to first treat the wood with a penetrating finish that will add to the surface hardness, and then cover the surface with a hard varnish.

Species

Each type of tree produces wood with unique characteristics. The technical term for a particular variety of tree is *species*. Listed in this section are the characteristics of some of the more common wood species that you will come across as

you begin wood finishing, and their finishing characteristics. There are hundreds of other species; the woods listed here are some of the ones commonly used to make furniture in the United States. The finishes recommended in this section are not the only ones you can use with a particular wood; they are just ones that work particularly well.

Alder (Illus. 1-12)
Hardwood
Closed-grained
Color: Light tan
Finishing characteristics: Alder accepts stains well, and is often used to imitate more expensive woods. Nicknamed "poor man's birch," it resembles birch when given a clear finish. When stained dark, it will look like walnut to the casual observer. A lot of unfinished furniture is made from alder. Since alder is not well known by the general public, it is often simply called "hardwood" by the furniture manufacturer. It is an easy wood to finish; practically any type of finish

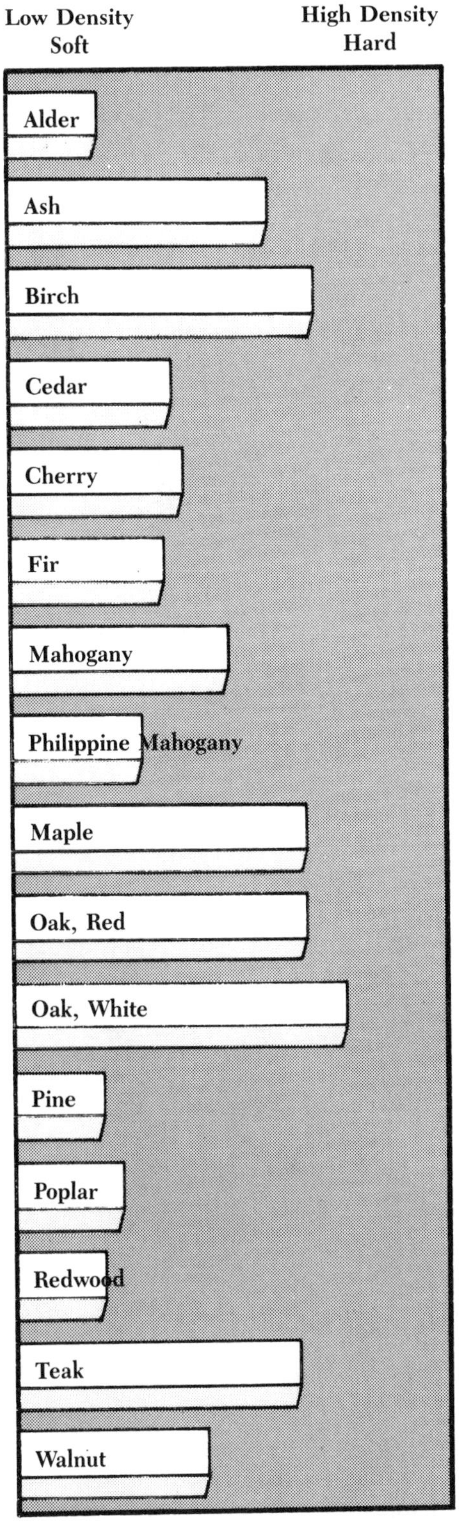

**Low Density
Soft** · **High Density
Hard**

Alder

Ash

Birch

Cedar

Cherry

Fir

Mahogany

Philippine Mahogany

Maple

Oak, Red

Oak, White

Pine

Poplar

Redwood

Teak

Walnut

Illus. 1-11. A wood's hardness can be measured by its density. This chart shows the density of various types of wood.

Illus. 1-12. Alder.

can be used on it. To bring out the nature color, use a clear, penetrating oil. Alder also looks good with a dark stain and satin varnish.

Ash (Illus. 1-13)
Hardwood
Open-grained, ring-porous
Color: Light tan
Finishing characteristics: Ash looks best with a clear finish or a light-colored stain. It is very

Illus. 1-13. Ash.

similar to oak in appearance but doesn't stain as well. Ash looks good when finished with a clear, penetrating oil or a thin coat of satin varnish. The pores can be left unfilled to show the natural texture of the ring-porous grain.

Birch (Illus. 1-14)
Hardwood
Closed-grained
Color: Heartwood reddish brown; sapwood almost white
Finishing characteristics: Birch stains very well. It can be stained to match many other types of wood. Birch plywood is often used as a cabinet back in cabinets made of other hardwoods; the birch can be stained to match the rest of the cabinet. White birch, which is cut from the sapwood, can be used when a very light finish is wanted.

The grain pattern in birch is not very pronounced, so use it when you want a uniform overall color. Birch looks good with a pastel finish; because of its smooth, hard surface, you can simply use a pastel penetrating oil finish and buff it to a soft luster. A clear satin varnish will bring out the natural color of birch. Birch also looks nice with a dark-walnut stain and varnish.

Illus. 1-14. Birch.

Cedar, Red, Eastern (Illus. 1-15)
Softwood
Closed-grained
Color: Red
Finishing characteristics: Red cedar has a strong, pleasant aroma. It repels moths, so it has been traditionally used for chests that store textiles. The interior of a cedar chest should be left unfinished to allow the aroma to escape from the wood. Cedar is usually not stained. A clear gloss varnish is the traditional choice as a finish for cedar. This brings out the natural beauty of the wood.

Illus. 1-15. Cedar, Red, Eastern.

Cherry (Illus. 1-16)
Hardwood
Closed-grained
Color: Reddish brown
Finishing characteristics: Cherry has a beautiful grain pattern and a fine texture that can be sanded to a smooth luster. For these reasons, it is a prime candidate for a clear penetrating oil finish. Several coats of penetrating finish will bring out the natural color and grain and can be buffed to a beautiful, soft luster. Cherry also finishes

well with other products. It stains well with medium-to-dark stains and can be given a high-gloss finish without filling.

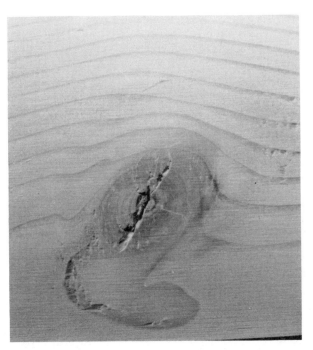

Illus. 1-17. Fir.

Illus. 1-16. Cherry.

Fir (Illus. 1-17)
Softwood
Closed-grained
Color: Reddish tan
Finishing characteristics: Fir is a difficult wood to finish well. Its summer wood is much denser than the spring wood. This makes it difficult to sand to a smooth, flat surface, because the softer parts of the grain sand away faster, leaving the summer wood raised slightly above the rest of the surface. It is also difficult to get an even color when staining. The spring wood absorbs a lot of stain, while the summer wood hardly absorbs any. This leads to a very pronounced grain pattern when dark stain is used.

One of the best finishes for fir is either a pastel or pickled finish. (See Chapter 11.) With these finishes, the characteristics listed above can be used to advantage. For a pickled finish, wire-brush the wood to further accentuate the grain, and then apply a pastel stain. Use satin varnish as the top coat. If you want to stain fir a dark color, treat the wood with wood conditioner first to help even out the color.

Mahogany (Illus. 1-18)
Hardwood
Open-grained, diffuse-porous
Color: Reddish brown
Finishing characteristics: Mahogany is one of the finest cabinetmaking woods. There are two varieties of mahogany: African and Honduran. African and Honduran mahogany are similar in appearance and have the same finishing characteristics.

Mahogany finishes very well. It is open-grained, but its pores are small, so they can be filled well with paste wood filler. It has a beautiful grain that is enhanced by reflective characteristics that change as the viewing angle changes. The traditional finish for mahogany is designed to enhance these reflective qualities. Stain the wood with a medium-dark stain. Fill the grain with paste wood filler. Use colored filler that matches the stain. Apply four thin coats of rubbing varnish. Wet-sand the finish with 600-grit sandpaper, and then rub it out with rubbing compound.

Illus. 1-18. Mahogany.

Illus. 1-19. Mahogany, Philippine.

Lacquer and shellac are also good top coats. For a satin finish, you can leave the grain open. For a high gloss, fill the grain with paste wood filler.

Mahogany, Philippine (Illus. 1-19)
Hardwood
Open-grained, diffuse-porous
Color: Reddish brown
Finishing characteristics: Philippine mahogany bears some resemblance to African mahogany, but it is not related. It is an inexpensive wood used in low-cost furniture and interior trim. It stains well, but its large pores make it difficult to achieve a smooth finish. It looks good when finished with a dark-walnut-colored penetrating oil. This leaves the texture of the wood showing, but gives the wood a soft sheen. If you want to varnish it, use a paste wood filler first. The pores are large, so the filler tends to pull out of them as you wipe it off. If this happens, work the filler back into the pores by rubbing the rag in a circular motion as you wipe off the excess. If the color of the filler is darker than the stain, the uniform pattern of pores will hide the grain pattern. It is better if the filler is exactly the same color as the lightest part of the grain after staining.

Maple (Illus. 1-20)
Hardwood
Closed-grain
Color: Light tan to almost white
Finishing characteristics: Because it is very hard and closed-grained, maple can be polished to a deep sheen with a penetrating oil finish. Use a clear oil or a penetrating oil that is combined with a light-colored stain. Sand in the oil with 600-grit sandpaper. Apply several coats of oil, and then wax and buff. Penetrating oil will bring out and slightly darken the natural color of the wood. If you want a clear finish that doesn't darken the wood, use lacquer. Varnish can be used, but it will darken the wood slightly. A pastel finish looks good on maple. Use a pastel penetrating oil. No top coat is needed. You can buff the oil to a soft luster.

Oak, Red (Illus. 1-21)
Hardwood
Open-grained, ring-porous
Color: Reddish tan
Finishing characteristics: Red oak has a beautiful grain and natural color. It looks very nice when

Illus. 1-20. Maple.

Illus. 1-21. Oak, Red.

oak accepts dark stains well. The stain will accumulate in the open pores, accentuating the grain pattern with a pleasing effect. A dark-colored penetrating oil is a good finish when you want a dark oak. The large pores of red oak are hard to fill with paste wood filler, so it is usually not a good choice for a high-gloss finish. Even after you have applied filler, some of the texture will show. If you want to varnish the wood, use satin varnish. You can apply filler before varnishing to make the pores less noticeable, but some texture will usually still show through in the top coat.

Oak, White (Illus. 1-22)

Hardwood
Open-grained, ring-porous
Color: Light tan
Finishing characteristics: Because of its light color, white oak is a good choice for pastel or pickled finishes. The white pigments in the finish will accumulate in the open grain, emphasizing the grain pattern. White oak stains well and can be stained any shade from light to dark. Its pores are large, but they are filled with small fibres. These fibres will trap filler, making it easier to fill the grain of white oak. If you carefully fill the

Illus. 1-22. Oak, White.

given a clear penetrating oil finish. Its large pores are concentrated in the darker parts of the grain pattern. The unfilled pores add a nice texture to the finish. If you want a darker color, red

grain with paste wood filler, you can give white oak a high-gloss finish. It looks particularly nice when rubbing varnish or lacquer is used and the finish is rubbed with rubbing compound.

Pine (Illus. 1-23)
Softwood
Closed-grained
Color: Light tan or amber
Finishing characteristics: Pine absorbs a stain unevenly; apply a wood conditioner before the stain to even out the absorption. Pine can be stained light or dark, but it looks best with light-to-medium shades. It works well with pastel finishes. Its light color and smooth texture produce a pleasing effect when a pastel rubbing oil is used.

Pine is often used to make Early American or "country" furniture. For these pieces, a distressed antique finish works well. Sand the wood smooth and round off sharp corners. Simulate the dents and gouges acquired over time by hitting the surface with a hard object such as a steel punch. For the top coat, either apply several coats of medium-colored penetrating oil or stain the wood with a medium-colored stain; then use orange shellac or a light brown varnish stain. Finally, apply a dark wax. Use #0000 steel wool to rub in the wax; then buff the surface with a soft cloth.

Illus. 1-23. Pine.

Poplar (Illus. 1-24)
Hardwood
Closed-grained
Color: Yellowish or greenish tan
Finishing characteristics: Poplar is often used in commercially made furniture and stained to simulate more expensive woods. It stains well and has a subtle grain. You can give it a satin-smooth finish by sanding in penetrating oil with 600-grit sandpaper. To darken the color, use a penetrating oil that includes a stain. High-gloss and satin varnish both work well when applied to poplar.

Illus. 1-24. Poplar.

Redwood (Illus. 1-25)
Softwood
Closed-grained
Color: Red
Finishing characteristics: Redwood is usually used for exterior furniture. It is very decay-resistant. If left unfinished, it will eventually age to a silver-grey color that is very attractive. If you want to preserve the original red color, give the wood an exterior penetrating oil finish. Don't use varnish for exterior furniture; it will eventually blister and peel.

Illus. 1-25. Redwood.

Teak (Illus. 1-26)

Hardwood
Open-grained, ring-porous
Color: Yellowish brown
Finishing characteristics: Teak is durable and water-resistant, so it is traditionally used for woodwork on ships and boats. It is also a fine furniture wood. Teak contains natural oils that can make it difficult to finish. The oils prevent surface coatings from adhering.

The best finish for teak is a penetrating oil finish. Some companies make a special teak oil that is formulated to be compatible with the natural oils in the wood. Teak can be finished with other products if the wood is carefully cleaned with solvent to remove the natural oils, but this is not recommended for beginners. If some oil remains, the finish can crack and peel later.

Walnut (Illus 1-27)

Hardwood
Open-grained, semi–ring-porous
Color: Heartwood dark brown; sapwood cream-colored
Finishing characteristics: Walnut is one of the easiest woods to finish. It has a hard surface, and beautiful color and grain. A clear penetrating oil finish is often the finish of choice for walnut. The natural color of the wood is so desirable that many times other woods are stained in an attempt to duplicate the color that is achieved by simply applying a clear finish to walnut.

Illus. 1-26. Teak.

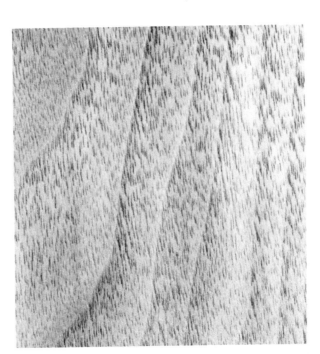

Illus. 1-27. Walnut.

Because the wood is hard, it can be highly polished; sanding in penetrating oil with 600-grit sandpaper will result in a satin-smooth polished surface. A final buffing with wax can produce a higher gloss. Stain can be used to even out color variations. In this case, choose a stain that closely matches the dark areas of the board.

When exposed to direct sunlight for many years, the natural color of walnut tends to lighten. The resulting color is pleasant. However, if you want to keep the original dark color on a piece of furniture that will be exposed to direct sunlight, stain the wood before applying a top coat. Even though it is an open-grained wood, the pores are small enough to be usually left unfilled. Filler should be used if you will be applying a high-gloss finish or plan on rubbing the top coat. One of the smoothest finishes possible is produced when lacquer or rubbing varnish is applied with rubbing compound.

Chapter 2

FINISHING TOOLS AND SUPPLIES

There are many different tools and supplies used in wood finishing. This chapter focuses on the basic tools and supplies that are needed to apply the finishes in this book. (See Illus. 2-1.) If you are interested in more advanced tools and supplies, consult my book *Wood Finisher's Handbook*.

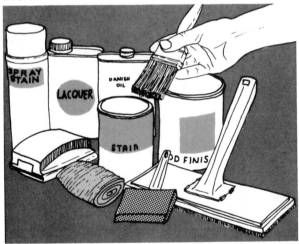

Illus. 2-1. Choosing the correct product or tool for the job is crucial to achieving a good finish. This chapter introduces you to the basic tools and supplies needed to apply the finishes described in this book.

Types of Finish

Wood finishes can be classified into two major categories: penetrating finishes and surface coatings. Penetrating finishes are thin-bodied and soak into the wood. Surface coatings are heavy-bodied and form a thin film on top of the wood surface. Both types have advantages and disadvantages. Each is described below.

Penetrating Finishes

Stains, penetrating oil finishes, and wood preservatives are examples of penetrating finishes. (See Illus. 2-2.) Penetrating finishes can be used under the top coat of a surface coating or by them-

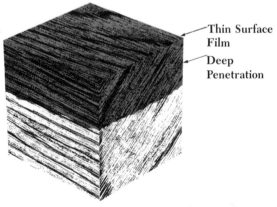

Thin Surface Film

Deep Penetration

Illus. 2-2. A penetrating finish soaks into the wood. The top surface of the wood is also the top surface of the finish. The penetrating finish strengthens and seals this top layer of wood, making a durable finish that is as smooth as the surface of the wood.

selves. When used as an undercoat, they serve to color the wood and prepare the surface for the final coats. When used by themselves, penetrat-

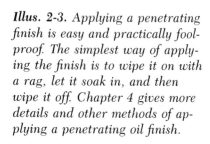

Illus. 2-3. Applying a penetrating finish is easy and practically fool-proof. The simplest way of applying the finish is to wipe it on with a rag, let it soak in, and then wipe it off. Chapter 4 gives more details and other methods of applying a penetrating oil finish.

ing finishes have several advantages. Since they soak into the wood, the natural surface texture of the wood still shows. If you want a natural texture, then a penetrating finish is needed. Penetrating finishes breathe better than surface coatings, so they will not blister or peel off.

A penetrating finish is easy to apply and practically foolproof, so it is an ideal finish for the novice. (See Illus. 2-3.)

Some penetrating finishes harden once they have soaked into the wood, increasing the surface hardness of the wood; others don't have this property.

The main disadvantage of a penetrating finish is that it leaves the surface of the wood exposed and more vulnerable to damage. However, a damaged penetrating finish is usually easier to repair than a surface coating.

Surface Coatings

Paint, varnish, lacquer, and shellac are all examples of surface coatings. They soak into the wood slightly, but most of the finish builds up as a film on the surface. (See Illus. 2-4.) They shed water better than a penetrating finish, and the film protects the wood surface from damage. For a smooth, glossy surface, use a surface coating. (See Illus. 2-5.)

Surface coatings are harder to apply than penetrating finishes, and they can blister and peel when moisture is present.

No matter what finishing products are being used, it is important to read and follow the directions that come with it. Pay particular attention to the safety recommendations. Also look at the directions to find out what other products are recommended as compatible with the one you intend to use. Not all finishing products are compatible with each other. If you apply a stain and then cover it with a varnish that is not compatible, you run the risk of discoloration or poor

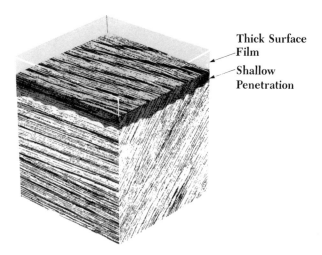

Thick Surface Film

Shallow Penetration

Illus. 2-4. A surface coating soaks into the wood slightly, but most of the material builds up as a film on the surface. It is harder to get a very smooth surface when using a surface coating, because brush marks and dust will create irregularities in the final surface.

Illus. 2-5. Varnish is usually applied with a brush. You must take care to apply an even coat, free from brush marks or dust.

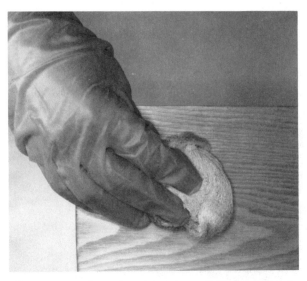

Illus. 2-6. A clean, lint-free piece of cloth is one of the most basic finishing tools. Cheesecloth works well. There are also specially made finishing cloths available that have a tighter weave. Household rags can also be used. If you use rags, make sure that they are clean and that they won't shed lint or make threads as you wipe the finish.

adhesion. The label will indicate the working temperature range of the product. If you apply a finish when the room temperature is too low, it will not dry properly. If the temperature is too high, the finish can dry too quickly and create a rough surface.

Finishing Tools

There are three main ways to apply finishing products: wiping, brushing, and spraying them on. This book covers procedures for wiping, brushing, and the use of aerosol spray cans. If you are interested in using spray equipment, refer to *Wood Finisher's Handbook*.

The only tool needed for wiping on a finish is a clean, lint-free cloth. (See Illus. 2-6.) Cheesecloth works well. Cheesecloth is available at stores that sell finishing supplies. There are also special finishing cloths available that have a tighter weave than cheesecloth. Ordinary household rags can also be used, as long as they don't leave lint on the finish.

Rags can become a fire hazard if they are disposed of improperly. After using a rag with an oil or flammable finish, immediately dispose of it in a covered metal container filled with water. Oily rags that are left in a pile can ignite spontaneously and cause a fire.

Brushed-on finishes can be applied with traditional brushes, foam brushes, pad applicators, and rollers. The traditional brush has been around for centuries. A brush is made from many small filaments that are attached to a handle. (See Illus. 2-7.) The filaments are arranged in groups and glued together at one end with a setting compound. A metal ferrule attaches the assembled filaments to the handle, which is made of wood or plastic.

The filaments used in brushes can be natural or synthetic. The most common type of natural brush filament is China bristle. China bristle is hog hair, and it is often simply called bristle.

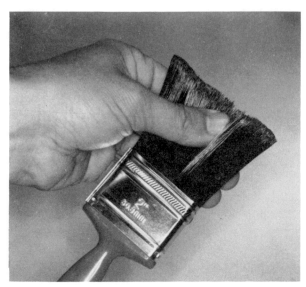

Illus. 2-7. The traditional type of brush has many individual hairs or filaments secured to a handle. It is still the best tool to use in some situations, but new products have surpassed the traditional brush for many jobs.

Nylon and polyester are the two most common types of synthetic filament used in brushes. Natural filaments are best for solvent-based finishes, while synthetic filaments are best for water-based finishes. Oil-based finishes can be applied with either type of brush.

Foam brushes look like a traditional brush, except that instead of filaments there is a single piece of foam plastic. (See Illus. 2-8.) Inside the

foam there is a plastic stiffener that helps the brush keep its shape. (See Illus. 2-9.) Foam brushes are inexpensive, so there is no need to clean them; simply discard them after use. But, disposability isn't their only advantage. They will usually produce better results in the hands of a novice than a traditional brush will. Foam

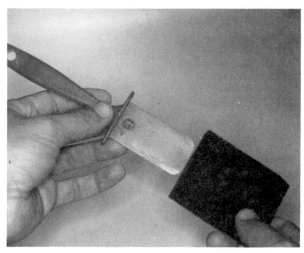

Illus. 2-9. A brush with a plastic stiffener is more effective when used to apply a finish than is a brush with an unstiffened piece of foam.

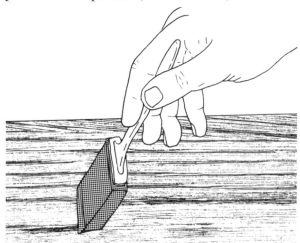

Illus. 2-8. The foam brush retains the shape of the traditional brush, but has a single piece of plastic foam instead of individual filaments.

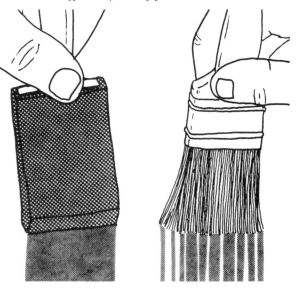

Illus. 2-10. For many jobs, the foam brush is superior to a traditional brush. In this comparison, note that the foam brush on the left holds more finish and produces fewer brush marks near the end of the stroke. The traditional brush on the right has run out of finish and has produced many brush marks at the same point in the stroke.

brushes spread the finish more evenly and leave fewer brush marks. (See Illus. 2-10.) For these reasons, use a foam brush for most finishing operations that will allow it. There are some cases when you just can't use a foam brush; these cases are described in the appropriate section of the book.

When the surface to be covered is large, use a roller or a pad applicator. Rollers are usually used with paint. Rollers tend to leave a textured surface. This is desirable when painting a surface like a wall, but for furniture and cabinets, a smoother finish is usually desired. Pad applica-

tors produce a smoother finish; they are especially well suited for applying stain to a large surface, but they can also be used for paint and varnish. (See Illus. 2-11.) They resemble a piece of short-napped carpet with a foam backing attached to a handle.

To use a pad applicator, fill a roller tray with the finishing product. Dip the pad into the finish, and then press it against the sloping section of the tray to remove the excess. (See Illus. 2-12.) Place the pad on the work and push or pull it across the surface in a long, even stroke with the grain direction.

Illus. 2-11. A pad applicator is a very efficient tool for applying finishing products to large surfaces. It produces a very smooth, even coat.

Illus. 2-12. Dip the pad applicator into the tray, and then squeeze out the excess on the sloping part of the tray.

Brush Care

Quality brushes can be reused for many years, if they are cared for correctly. Even disposable brushes can be reused several times. The key is to clean the brush thoroughly after use. With water-based products, it is very simple to clean a brush. Place it in a container of water and work the brush against the side of the container until most of the finish is washed out; then hold the brush under running water to rinse out the remaining material. Pat the brush dry with a rag and hang it up.

You must use solvents to clean brushes that are used with finishes that are not water-based. Paint thinner can be used to remove most oil-based products from brushes. Lacquer thinner is used to remove lacquer, and alcohol to remove shellac. Start by placing the brush in a container of thinner. Wipe the brush against the side of the container to work out the material. (See Illus. 2-13.) When most of the finish has been worked out of the brush, dry the brush with a rag. Next, place

Illus. 2-13. The first step in cleaning a brush is to use the appropriate thinner to remove the remaining material from the brush. For water-based finishes, use water; for oil-based products, paint thinner; for shellac, alcohol; and for lacquer, lacquer thinner.

it under running water and lather it with a bar of hand soap. (See Illus. 2-14.) Rub the bristles between your fingers while running water over them. Stop when you have removed all of the remaining soap.

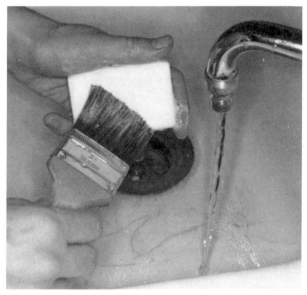

Illus. 2-14. After you have cleaned the brush as thoroughly as possible by rinsing it in thinner, wash it under running water. Work up a lather with a bar of hand soap. This will remove the last traces of the finishing product.

Now, pat the brush dry and hang it up. You can ensure that a brush will retain its shape as it dries by wrapping it in a piece of paper. Fold the paper to make an envelope that holds the bristles in shape. (See Illus. 2-15.) Place a rubber band around the paper. (See Illus. 2-16.)

When you are working on a project for several days in a row, you can prevent the finish from hardening in the brush overnight by squeezing out most of the remaining finish with a rag and then sealing the brush in a plastic sandwich bag. This procedure also works for disposable brushes. (See Illus. 2-17.) Keeping the brushes in plastic bags ensures that you can use the same disposable brush for several coats of finish. If the foam starts to deteriorate, replace the brush. Tiny bits of foam in the finish can make unsightly bumps.

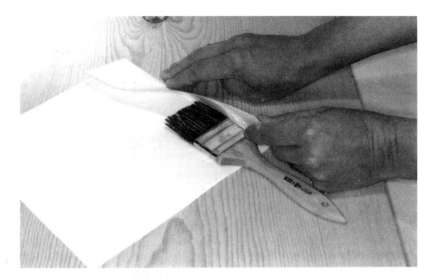

Illus. **2-15.** *Now put the brush away to dry. If you fold a paper envelope around the bristles while they are wet, it will help them hold their shapes.*

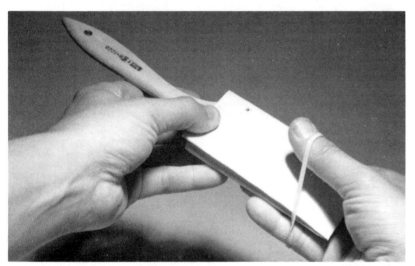

Illus. **2-16.** *Use a rubber band to hold the paper envelope on the brush. Place the rubber band around the metal ferrule so that it won't squeeze the bristles.*

Illus. **2-17.** *You can store a brush in a plastic bag overnight to avoid cleaning it. Squeeze out most of the remaining finishing material with a rag first, and then seal the brush in the bag. This way, it is only necessary to clean the brush once—when you are through with the project.*

Spray Cans

Many finishing products come in spray cans. (See Illus. 2-18.) When the project is small, you can use spray cans to get professional results without spray equipment. (See Illus. 2-19.) Spraying is particularly useful when the project has many small details that would make brushing difficult. (See Illus. 2-20.) Spray cans are not hard to use, but the proper techniques are needed to get good results.

Always shake the can before use. Most products will have an agitator ball, which sounds like a small marble moving inside the can. When you first start shaking the can, the ball will usually be stuck in the sediment at the bottom. When it shakes loose, you will hear it rattle around. The purpose of the agitator ball is to stir up the pigments that settle to the bottom of the can. Some clear finishes don't need an agitator ball because they don't contain any pigments. Shake the can for the time recommended on the label, usually about one minute. Also shake the can occasionally between strokes as you use the product.

To spray, hold the can about 6 inches from the surface. (See Illus. 2-21.) If you hold the can too close, then drips and runs are likely to form. If you hold it too far away, the finish will start to dry before it hits the wood. This will result in a rough surface.

Start to spray just before you reach the edge of the project, and move the can in a straight line to the other side. Stop spraying just after the can is past the other edge. Try to keep the can the same distance from the surface all the time. (See Illus. 2-22.) Move the can at a steady pace; the exact speed is a matter of judgment. The objective is to spray a light coat that will cover the surface. If you move too slowly, the coat will be too thick and drips and runs will develop. If you move too fast, the coat will be too thin. It is better to be slightly fast, because you can always go back over the surface again.

Drips and runs caused by going too slowly are harder to deal with. If drips and runs do develop,

Illus. 2-18. Most finishing products are available in spray cans. Spraying the finish produces a professional-looking smooth finish that is free from brush marks.

Illus. 2-19. You can finish small projects like this clock by using spray cans, and get professional-looking results.

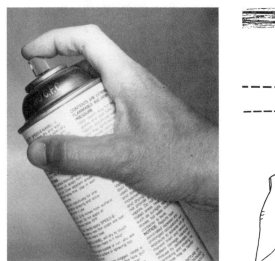

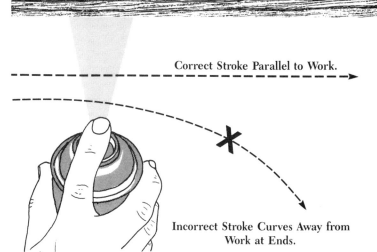

Illus. 2-20. This project would be difficult to finish with brushes or rags because of the intricate details. Applying the finish with a spray can ensures an even coat.

Correct Stroke Parallel to Work.

Incorrect Stroke Curves Away from Work at Ends.

Illus. 2-21 (above left). Hold a spray can with your thumb on one side, index finger on the spray head, and the rest of your fingers on the other side of the can. Keep the can as close to vertical as possible when spraying vertical surfaces. For horizontal surfaces, tilt the can between 30 and 45 degrees. For most products, you will get the best results if the can is held at a constant 6 inches from the work through the stroke. Always read the directions on the can, and use the distance specified there if it differs from 6 inches. Illus. 2-22 (above right). Always move the can in a straight line parallel to the work. If you are not careful, it is easy to swing the can in an arc. This will result in a heavy coat in the center of the stroke and a thin coat near the edges.

wipe them off while they are still wet. Use a clean rag. Then spray a little more in the same area. After the coat is dry, you will probably need to sand the area with 220-grit sandpaper before applying another coat. As with any finishing product, follow the directions that appear on the can.

Spray cans are designed to operate best when they are held straight up. This is fine for vertical surfaces, but for horizontal surfaces the can must be tipped. The lip of the can has a small inked dot. Turn the nozzle so that it points to this dot. This lines up the nozzle with the end of the feed tube. The tube is bent so that it will pick up the fluid even when the can is tilted. (See Illus. 2-23.)

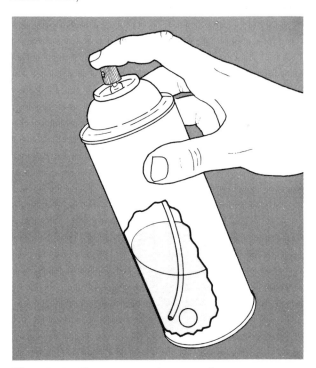

Illus. 2-23. *This cutaway drawing of a spray can shows the bent feed tube that allows you to tilt the can downwards to spray horizontal surfaces. The location of the bent end is marked on the top of the can with an inked dot on the rim near the nozzle. Twist the nozzle so that the hole is lined up with this mark.*

There are several types of spray nozzle. The two most common types are shown in Illus. 2-24. The first type produces a round spray pattern. This is the type most often used, and it produces equally good results regardless of the direction of travel. The second type is designed to operate more like a professional spray gun. It produces a fan pattern. You must turn the nozzle to adjust the spray pattern for either side-to-side or up-and-down motion. The fan pattern covers a larger area in one sweep and generally produces a more even finish.

The nozzles on spray cans frequently become clogged. This won't usually happen with a new can. A nozzle can become clogged once you have used some of the finish, let the can sit for several months, and then try to use the can again. One of

Standard Spray Pattern

Fan Spray Pattern

Twist Nozzle to Change Fan Orientation.

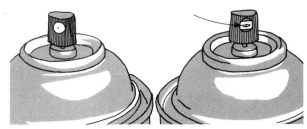

Illus. 2-24. *A standard spray nozzle produces a round spray pattern. With this pattern, it doesn't matter in which direction you move the can. A fan-pattern nozzle uses the elongated pattern professionals prefer. You must turn the tip of this nozzle so that the indicator line is parallel to the direction of the stroke.*

the best solutions is to replace the clogged nozzle with a nozzle from an empty can. Make sure that the nozzles are of the same type. Don't try to clean the nozzle with a pin; this usually doesn't work, and, even it if does, the hole made is usually too big and a poor spray pattern is produced. Never poke anything into the valve on the can! This can cause a serious injury.

The most common place for the nozzle to clog is in a small slit on the stem. Remove the nozzle from the can and run your fingernail through the slit. This will unclog most nozzles. (See Illus. 2-25.)

Abrasives

Abrasives are used to smooth the wood before a finish is applied, and to prepare the finished surface for additional coats. The three most common types of abrasive used in wood finishing are sandpaper, steel wool, and synthetic finishing pads.

Sandpaper is technically called a coated abrasive, because small abrasive particles are coated

Illus. 2-25. *There is a small slit on the stem of the nozzle. This slit is often the area on the nozzle that gets clogged. Use your fingernail to clean out the slit, and the nozzle will usually work fine again.*

on a sheet of backing paper. (See Illus. 2-26.) Sandpaper comes in many grades based on the size of the abrasive particles. For wood finishing uses, 80 grit is the coarsest sandpaper usually used. For bare wood sanding, 320-grit sandpaper is the finest used. (Coarse sandpaper has larger grit particles than fine sandpaper.) Finer grades, such as 400-grit or 600-grit sandpaper, are used to smooth a finished surface.

Sandpaper is used to prepare the wood for a finish. This is covered in detail in Chapter 3. Sandpaper can also be used between coats of a finish to smooth out imperfections and rough up

the surface to make the next coat adhere better. One disadvantage of using sandpaper on a finished surface is that it clogs up with residue from the finish. This can be prevented by using wet or dry sandpaper and a lubricant such as water or oil.

Steel wool has been a traditional favorite of wood finishers for use between coats of finish. There are two reasons for this: Steel wool won't clog like sandpaper, and, because it is flexible, it will conform to surface irregularities. (See Illus. 2-27.) With the introduction of modern water-based finishes, steel wool has become less useful, because the small steel particles it leaves can react to water-based finishes by producing discolored areas in the finish. Steel wool leaves a large number of small steel particles on the surface. All of these particles must be removed or they will create problems in the next coat of finish.

Steel wool comes in several grades based on the size of the steel strands. The coarsest grade used in wood finishing is #2. It is used to remove stubborn finishes with stripper. A finer grade that is used to remove the residue left when stripping an old finish is #0. For preparing a finished surface between coats, use #00 or #000. The finest grade is #0000. It is used to buff the top coat of a finish to give it a smooth satin luster.

Synthetic finishing pads are a synthetic substitute for steel wool. (See Illus. 2-28.) They can be used with water-based finishes. They will last

Illus. 2-26. *Sandpaper is used extensively in wood finishing. It comes in various grades. The grit size is indicated by a number printed on the back of the sheet. A sanding block is essential also. It can simply be a shop-made block of wood, or you can use a commercially made one.*

Illus. 2-27. Steel wool is a traditional favorite of wood finishers. It is used to smooth the finish between coats. It won't clog like sandpaper, and it will conform to intricate shapes. The grade of steel wool is indicated by a number on the package. Steel wool sheds steel particles on the project. You must thoroughly remove these particles or they will cause bumps in the finish. Do not use steel wool with water-based finishes, because even a tiny particle of steel left on the surface will cause a dark rust spot when a water-based finish is applied.

Illus. 2-28. A synthetic finishing pad is a modern substitute for steel wool. It works just like steel wool, but lasts longer, won't shed particles on the project, and can be used with water-based products.

much longer than steel wool, and they don't shed small particles as steel wool does. The coarsest type is called a stripping pad and corresponds roughly to #2 steel wool. Finer pads are called finishing pads and can be used between finishing coats, like #00 or #000 steel wool.

Synthetic finishing pads are very useful. They simplify the finishing process, because you can use them between finish coats without a lubricant and eliminate the clogging problems associated with sandpaper. They are flexible and will conform to the small irregularities in the surface. When they do become clogged with finish residue, you can rinse them out and reuse them. Since they won't react to water-based finishes, they can be used with the new strippers and finishes when steel wool cannot be used. They

are also useful with traditional finishes and can be used in most instances when steel wool would be used.

Safety Techniques

Finishing products can be toxic and flammable. Be sure to follow all the safety precautions that the product manufacturer recommends on the label. Always wear protective gloves when your skin might come in contact with the finishing product. Wear goggles if there is a chance that the product could get splashed into your eyes. (See Illus. 2-29.) Work outside when possible, or at least in a well-ventilated area.

Illus. 2-29. Most finishing products will cause severe eye injury if they get splashed in your eyes. Wear goggles whenever there is a chance that something may get in your eyes.

Illus. 2-30. Sanding dust can cause lung problems. Wear a dust mask to filter out the dust as you sand or do other operations that create dust.

Fumes can be toxic. An ordinary dust mask is not sufficient protection against toxic fumes; it is only useful for keeping dust particles caused by sanding out of your lungs. (See Illus. 2-30.) When working with any product or material that emits toxic fumes, use a respirator that is designed to protect you against them. (See Illus. 2-31.) In most cases, avoid highly toxic material and use another product that is less toxic.

When using flammable material, be sure to avoid doing anything that could start a fire. Don't work around any appliance that has a pilot light or electrical devices that may produce sparks. Whenever possible, use one of the newer products that is nonflammable instead of the older, flammable type.

Illus. 2-31. A respirator has special filters that will protect you from some types of solvent fumes. Be sure to read the directions that come with the respirator to find out what material it can handle. Good ventilation is always necessary when you use materials that have harmful fumes.

Chapter 3

WOOD PREPARATION

Wood preparation is one of the most important steps in wood finishing. (See Illus. 3-1.) If the wood is not smooth, none of the later steps will compensate for the lack of adequate surface preparation. The instructions in this chapter deal with new wood that has not been previously finished. For instructions on preparing previously finished wood after the old finish has been stripped off, refer to Chapter 12.

Wood preparation begins before the project is even built. After lumber is cut, it has a rough surface. The surface has to be smoothed before the wood can be used for a project. Advanced

Illus. 3-1. *Before you begin to apply any finishing product, you must first smooth and prepare the wood surface. Nail holes and defects must be filled and the wood sanded smooth.*

woodworkers sometimes buy rough-cut lumber and surface it themselves, but beginning woodworkers should buy lumber that has been surfaced at the mill. This is called S4S lumber, meaning surfaced on four sides. When using S4S lumber, your first step consists of sanding it.

If you are building the project yourself, do some of the initial sanding before assembling the project. If you are finishing a piece of unfinished furniture, this initial sanding has been done for you and you can proceed to the final sanding steps. Many experienced woodworkers prefer to do the initial work with planes and scrapers, and then finish with fine grades of sandpaper. If you are interested in using planes and scrapers, refer to *Wood Finisher's Handbook*. In this basic book, only the procedures for using sandpaper are described.

Wood Putty

After you have assembled the project, use wood putty to fill nail holes and defects in the wood, such as cracks and knotholes. For nail holes and other small defects, use the point of a knife to apply the putty. (See Illus. 3-2.) Do not smear much putty outside the area of the hole; this putty can seal the wood and cause it to stain lighter than the surrounding wood. Leave the putty slightly higher than the wood surface, be-

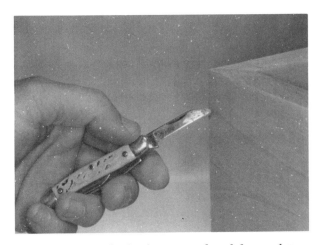

Illus. 3-2. A pocketknife is a good tool for applying putty to nail holes. Just use a little putty on the point of the knife. Don't spread the putty around outside the hole, because it can cause a light spot when stain is applied.

cause it will shrink as it dries. Larger defects like cracks and knotholes can also be filled with wood putty.

Use a putty knife to apply the putty. (See Illus. 3-3.) If the defect is deep, you may have to apply a second coat of putty after the first one is dry. This is because the putty may shrink below the surface as it dries. When the wood putty is dry, sand it smooth with 80- or 100-grit sandpaper and then proceed to sand the rest of the project.

It is not always necessary to fill small defects before finishing. There are products that are colored to match many popular shades of stain that can be used to fill nail holes and small defects after the finish has been applied. One such product is a filler stick. A filler stick is like a wax crayon. (See Illus. 3-4.) Rub the point of the stick over the defect until enough of the putty rubs off to fill the hole. Rub off the excess putty with a rag. (See Illus. 3-5.) Colored putty is also available in a paste form. (See Illus. 3-6.) Apply the putty to the hole, and then wipe off the excess with a rag.

Illus. 3-4. A filler stick can be used to fill nail holes and small defects after the finish has been applied. The sticks are available in many colors to match most finishes.

Illus. 3-3. Use a putty knife to apply wood putty to larger defects like this crack in a knot.

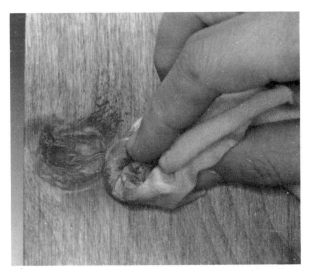

Illus. 3-5. After rubbing the filler stick over the hole, wipe off the excess with a rag.

Illus. 3-6. This type of colored putty is a paste. It is usually applied after the stain but before the top coat. Put on a plastic glove and use the tip of your finger to press the putty into the hole. Then wipe off the excess with a rag.

When the project is completely assembled before the finish is applied, use wood putty to fill all nail holes and defects before applying the finish. Filler sticks and colored putty are most useful when some assembly of the project is necessary after the finish has been applied; then you can fill the necessary fastener holes with colored putty to hide them.

Sandpaper

There are several types of sandpaper. The specific type you will buy will be determined by the abrasive grit size, abrasive material, and backing material needed for the job. These three factors are described below.

Grit Size

The size of the individual pieces of grit on the sandpaper determines whether the sandpaper is coarse or fine. Large-grit particles will cut fast but leave large, visible scratches on the surface of the wood. Small-grit particles will cut more slowly, but they leave small scratches that are less noticeable. The size of the grit is designated by a number. The number represents the number of holes found per square inch in a mesh screen used to sort the abrasive particles. For use in wood finishing, sandpaper in grit sizes ranging from 80 to 600 is available. A low number means that the grit is coarse, and a high number means that the grit is fine.

The mesh-screen method used to sort the abrasive particles allows some variation in their size. A few particles that are smaller than average and a few that are bigger than average will be included on the sandpaper. The small ones aren't much of a problem; they just decrease the cutting efficiency of the abrasive. Abrasive particles that are too large, however, can make scratches. Fortunately, most sandpaper is fairly uniform, and for most uses, you won't need anything better. When you need the smoothest possible surface, however, there is a new type of abrasive available called Micron-graded abrasive. This abrasive material is the same as used in traditional sandpaper, but the method of sorting the particles for size is more accurate, so there are fewer off-size particles.

Types of Abrasive

Originally, sandpaper was made only from natural minerals, such as flint and garnet. Now synthetic materials are also used. Flint paper is still available, but its only advantage is that it is inexpensive. It will wear out sooner than the synthetics, so it is not really cheaper to use. Garnet is a natural mineral that is used to make sandpaper. It is still widely used. It isn't as hard as the synthetic abrasives, but it is friable; that is, the abrasive particles tend to fracture, or break, while the sandpaper is being used. This continually exposes new sharp edges and makes the paper cut fast.

Aluminum oxide is the most widely used abrasive for most woodworking uses. It is a synthetic abrasive that is very hard and durable, so the sandpaper lasts longer. It is most often used on bare wood. Silicon carbide is another synthetic abrasive. It is used more often to sand between coats of finish, because it is friable. As you sand, the grit tends to fracture; this produces a new sharp edge continually, so the paper cuts clean and fast.

Use aluminum oxide sandpaper for all bare-wood sanding, and silicon-carbide paper when sanding between finish coats.

Backing

The abrasive particles can be attached to several types of backing. The most common is paper. Paper backing comes in several weights. The lightest paper is A weight. This is usually called finishing paper. The heaviest paper generally used in wood finishing is D weight. In most cases, you don't have much choice as to the weight of the backing paper; the coarser grades can be found on heavier paper, and the finer grades on light paper.

The way the grit is attached to the paper is important, and here you do have a choice. If the entire surface of the paper is coated with abrasives, it is called closed-coat paper. When there are spaces around the grit particles, it is called open-coat paper. Closed-coat paper cuts faster, but clogs up when used on softwoods or when you are sanding between coats of a finish. Open-coat paper doesn't clog as quickly, so it is useful when clogging is likely. Also available is sandpaper with a special anti-clogging coating.

There are other types of backing besides paper. Cloth-backed abrasives are effective when durability and flexibility are needed. Cloth-backed abrasives are more expensive than paper-backed ones, but they will last longer when being used to sand irregularly shaped objects. They are also useful with power sanders, because they resist tearing. Screen-backed abrasives are useful when clogging is a major problem. The abrasive is coated on a fibreglass screen.

Plastic film is a new type of backing that has many advantages. It is strong like cloth, and it actually makes the abrasive cut better. With paper- and cloth-backed abrasives, some of the abrasive particles are pressed into the backing, where they are not effective. With the plastic film, all of the abrasive particles are on the surface, where they will cut most effectively. Plastic film is also uniform in thickness and is waterproof.

When sanding the final coats of a finish, it is often useful to use water as a lubricant. This makes the sandpaper cut better and prevents clogging. When using water as a sanding lubricant, use wet-or-dry sandpaper. The abrasives in wet-or-dry sandpaper are attached with waterproof glue. The abrasives in ordinary sandpaper are attached with a water-soluble glue, so if the sandpaper gets wet, the particles will fall off.

Sanding Technique

The purpose of the initial sanding is to remove any irregularities in the wood surface. The sanding steps that follow the initial sanding remove the scratches left by it and produce a smooth surface for the finish.

The wood dust produced during sanding can be irritating and damaging to your lungs. Wear a dust mask while sanding, and clean up the accumulated dust frequently.

When building a project, do the initial sanding after the parts are cut, but before assembly. At this stage, the objective is to remove the irregularities left by the mill when the lumber was surfaced and any dents or scratches that have occurred during handling. If you are using a good grade of plywood, and the initial sanding was done at the mill, skip this step unless there is some damage to the wood that has to be sanded out.

Use a block of wood as a sanding block. A

Illus. **3-7.** *Cut the sheet of sandpaper into fourths to fit a sanding block that is $3 \times 5 \times \frac{3}{4}$ inches.*

piece of hardwood that is $3 \times 5 \times \frac{3}{4}$ inches makes a good sanding block. A block of this size will fit into a fourth of a standard-size sheet of sandpaper. (See Illus. 3-7.) The sanding block must have a smooth, flat surface, so choose a piece of wood that doesn't have any bumps or gouges on it. To further flatten the surface of the sanding block, lay a piece of 100-grit sandpaper grit side up on a flat surface and hold it in place with one hand. With the other hand, rub the sanding block back and forth over the sandpaper until the face of the block is smooth and flat.

The first grade of sandpaper used depends upon the condition of the boards you are sanding. If they are already fairly smooth, start with 100-grit sandpaper. If there are many defects to sand out, start with 80 grit. If you are using plywood that has been sanded at the mill, you may be able to go directly to 150 grit.

Fold the sandpaper around the block and hold it in place with your thumb on one side and your fingers on the other. (See Illus. 3-8.) Place the block on the board with its folded edge facing the end of the board. If you sand with the folded edges facing the sides of the board, then the edge of the paper can get caught on a sliver of wood and tear. Press down slightly on the block and move it back and forth in long strokes with the grain of the wood. (See Illus. 3-9.) Don't sand across the grain, because the scratches will be highly visible and difficult to remove.

Sand the boards with the first grade of sand-

paper until all of the scratches, nicks, and roughness have been removed. Then switch to the next grade of sandpaper. So, for example, if you start with 80-grit sandpaper, switch to 100 grit and sand the surface again before assembling the project. Do the rest of the sanding after the project is assembled. If you are working on a piece of unfinished furniture, you usually don't need to do the initial sanding; most of the time, the project has been sanded with 100-grit sandpaper at the factory.

When the initial sanding has been finished, the boards should be flat and smooth. The only job remaining is to remove the coarse scratches

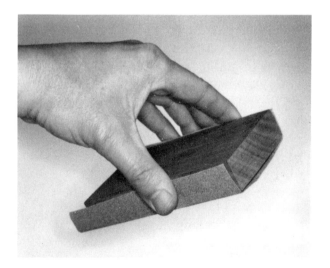

Illus. **3-8.** *Fold the sandpaper around the block and hold it in place with your thumb and fingers.*

Illus. 3-9. Sand with the grain direction. Hold the sanding block so that a folded edge of the sandpaper faces forward. This will prevent the paper from snagging on a sliver of wood and tearing.

left by the initial sanding and smooth out any roughness that occurred during assembly. For this job, use a flexible sanding block. You can buy sanding blocks made of rubber or plastic that work well. (See Illus. 3-10.) These commercial sanding blocks have pegs on which to secure the sandpaper, and a comfortable handle. (See Illus. 3-11.) These features make a commercial sanding block a good investment, but you can also make your own padded sanding block by gluing a piece of cork or felt to a block of wood. (See Illus. 3-12.)

Attach a piece of 150-grit sandpaper to the block and sand all of the surfaces on the project. Sand one spot just long enough to replace the coarse scratches left by the 100-grit sandpaper with the finer scratches left by the 150-grit sandpaper. At this stage, also slightly round the sharp edges of the project by holding the block at an angle and making a few passes along the edge. Unless you want the look of a time-worn edge for an antique reproduction, don't sand the corners too much. Just remove the sharp corner, but leave it looking crisp and square.

After you have sanded the entire project with 150-grit sandpaper, switch to 180 grit and repeat the process. Remember that at this stage there is no need to sand hard or long; just sand enough to remove the scratches left by the preceding grade of sandpaper.

It is important to remove all of the sanding dust from the preceding sanding step before proceeding with the next grade of sandpaper. As you

sand, some of the abrasives will break off the sandpaper and remain in the sanding dust. If you don't remove the dust, these abrasives will continue to scratch the surface as you sand with the finer sandpaper. A soft-bristled brush works well for removing the dust. (See Illus. 3-13.) A vacuum with a brush attachment works even better. (See Illus. 3-14.) It also has the advantage of removing the dust from the work area and keeping it out of the air.

Next, use 220-grit sandpaper. For most finishes, this is the finest grade you will need to use on the bare wood. For a very smooth surface when using a penetrating oil finish, sand the bare

Illus. 3-10. A commercial sanding block has a rubber pad between the sandpaper and the block. The padded type of sanding block is best for the stages after the initial sanding.

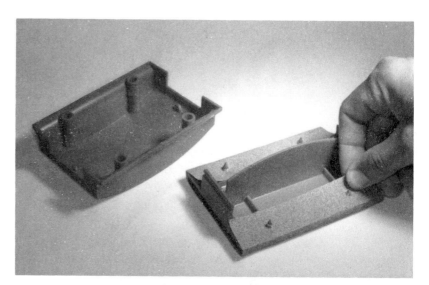

Illus. 3-11. *This commercial sanding block has pegs on which to secure the sandpaper. When the handle is snapped in place, the sandpaper is held securely on the block.*

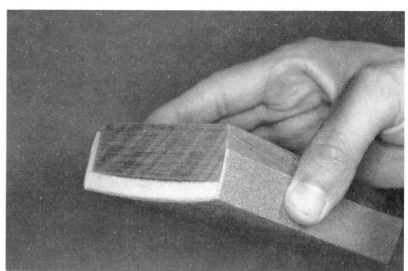

Illus. 3-12. *You can make a padded sanding block by gluing a piece of cork or felt to the bottom of a wood block.*

Illus. 3-13. *A soft bristle brush can be used to remove the sanding dust.*

Illus. 3-14. A shop vacuum with a brush attachment is an efficient way to remove sanding dust.

wood one more time with 320-grit sandpaper before applying the finish.

After the final sanding, carefully remove all of the sanding dust. Use a vacuum with a brush attachment for the best results. Immediately before applying the first coat of finish, wipe the surface of the project with a tack cloth. (See Illus. 3-15.) A tack cloth is a piece of cheesecloth that has been treated to make it attract and trap dust. Tack cloths are inexpensive and available at most stores that sell finishing supplies. When one area of the cloth becomes coated with dust, refold the cloth to expose a fresh surface. Though it is possible to make your own tack cloths, this is not a good idea. Commercial tack cloths work better, and a shop-made tack cloth can be a fire hazard.

Power Sanders

Sanding is one of the most laborious jobs in woodworking. If you are finishing a large project, you will probably want to use a power sander for some of the sanding. A belt sander is a good choice for the initial sanding. (See Illus. 3-16.) It has a continuous abrasive belt that is stretched between two rollers. One roller is connected to the motor, and the other is spring-loaded to apply tension to the belt. A belt sander is good to use for the initial sanding because it will remove a lot of wood quickly, so that you can sand out the defects quickly. However, this can have a disadvantage for beginners who are not careful. Keep the sander moving and sand uniformly over the entire surface of the board. If you leave the sander in one spot too long, you can create a dip in the surface. If you are sanding plywood, it is possible to sand completely through the face, exposing the underlying ply.

Even with the drawbacks just described, a belt sander is probably the best type of sander to use for the initial sanding. With some practice, you

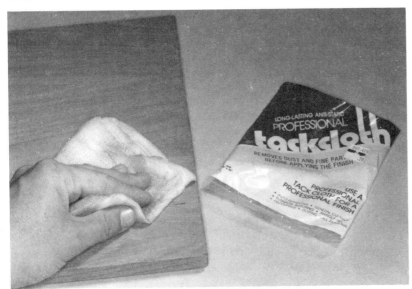

Illus. 3-15. Use a tack cloth to remove the last traces of dust just before you apply the finish.

will get the feel of how to handle it. Since the belt travels in only one direction, the sanding marks left by the belt sander will be along the grain, as long as the sander is held parallel to the grain. This is important when coarse sandpaper is being used, because any cross-grain scratches will be very difficult to remove.

Belts for the belt sander are available in the finer grades needed for the remaining sanding steps, so that all of the sanding can be done with the belt sander. And, unlike the orbital sander described in the following paragraph, a belt sander does not leave swirl marks. No matter which sander you use, you will have to hand-sand in places that can't be reached with the power sander.

The other major type of sander is the orbital sander. (See Illus. 3-17.) It leaves small swirl marks that can be very noticeable when the sandpaper is coarse, but these marks tend to disappear when the sandpaper is fine.

Orbital sanders have a padded base and are well suited for sanding with the finer grades of sandpaper. They remove wood more slowly than belt sanders and are easier to control, so many wood finishers prefer to use them. Orbital sanders use standard sandpaper. Simply cut the paper to size and attach it to the sander.

Illus. 3-16. A belt sander sands quickly, and its sanding marks appear in a straight line with the grain of the wood. It is a very good tool to use for the initial stages of sanding.

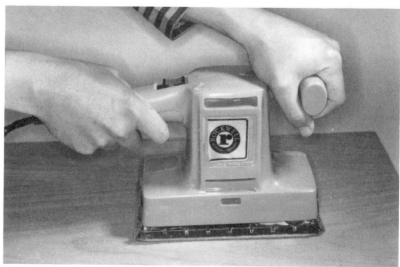

Illus. 3-17. An orbital sander sands more slowly than a belt sander, and is easy to control. It is good for use with finer grades of sandpaper. Its main disadvantage is that the sanding marks are circular, so small swirl marks can show up in the finished surface. Newer, random-orbit models are less likely to leave swirl marks.

Chapter 4
APPLYING A RUBBED OIL FINISH

A rubbed oil finish can be one of the most beautiful finishes applied to wood. (See Illus. 4-1.) It is highly recommended for beginners because it is a penetrating finish, while other finishes like varnish or shellac are surface coatings. When you are working with a surface coating, the quality of the final finished surface is determined by how skillfully you have applied the final coat. Brush marks, dust, runs, and drips can mar the finish. A penetrating finish soaks into the wood, so the visible top surface is the surface of the wood itself. This means that if you have sanded the wood to a smooth surface, the top coat will be smooth. Also, a penetrating finish enhances the natural color and texture of the wood without obscuring the natural grain or color variations. (See Illus. 4-2.)

Penetrating finishes can be used in almost all applications. The main disadvantage is that there is more hand labor involved than if a surface coat is used. Also, penetrating finishes may not provide as much protection to the underlying wood as a surface coating would in some situations. When minor damage occurs to a surface coating, the finish is damaged but not the wood below. When a penetrating finish is used, the wood surface is exposed to any abrasions that might occur. However, it is probably easier to repair a damaged penetrating oil finish than it is to repair a damaged surface coating. Most penetrating finishes are made for interior use, but some are formulated to stand the extreme conditions of exterior use.

Penetrating finishes leave the texture of the wood visible on its surface. This is an advantage when you want that type of look. If you are after a smooth, glossy surface, however, then use a surface coating. Also, since the texture of the wood is exposed, dirt can get pressed into the surface more easily. If the project will be used in an extremely dirty environment, then a surface coating would be a better choice.

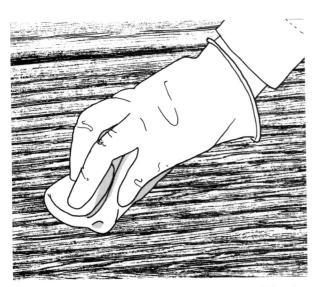

Illus. 4-1. The rubbed-oil finish is a beautiful finish that can be applied with a rag and is practically foolproof.

Illus. 4-2. This inlaid box is finished with a hand-rubbed oil. The finish highlights the color and character of the wood without obscuring the design.

Penetrating finishes protect the wood by soaking into the top layer of the board and then hardening. This produces a layer of wood on the surface that is harder than the original surface and is moisture-resistant. Since the finish is not a surface coating, it will not chip, blister, or peel. Minor damage isn't that noticeable because the finish extends below the surface of the board.

Types of Penetrating Oil Finish

There are many types of penetrating oil finish available that range from dull to high-luster finish. You can use a clear finish that will bring out the natural color of the wood or use a product that also contains a stain that colors the wood. Because of the wide range of penetration finishes available, virtually any look can be achieved when the right product is used.

Many penetrating oils contain tung oil. This is a natural oil obtained from the nut of the tung tree. Tung oil reacts with oxygen from the air to form a natural plastic material that is resistant to alcohol, fruit acids, acetone, and carbonated drinks. Pure tung oil is difficult to apply, so it is blended with other ingredients to make a finish that can be applied easily.

Natural tung oil can be modified to produce a harder, glossier surface. The modified oil is called cooked tung oil. Manufacturers blend cooked oil with natural oil and other ingredients to produce several types of penetrating finish. The finish you choose depends on the amount of gloss desired.

A low-luster finish penetrates deeply into the wood. It will darken the natural color of the wood and bring out natural color variations. It has practically no gloss and allows the natural texture of the wood to show. A low-luster finish is very easy to apply and dries rapidly. Repeated coats of this finish soak into the wood and don't build much additional gloss.

A medium-lustre finish doesn't penetrate as deeply into the wood, but it cures to a harder surface. Additional coats build up to create a satin gloss. Some surface texture is hidden, but most of it is still visible. A medium-luster finish is slightly more difficult to apply than a low-luster finish, but it is still practically foolproof.

A high-gloss finish requires more skill to apply than low- and medium-gloss finishes. Each additional coat builds the gloss and fills some surface texture. If the finish starts to get tacky (somewhat sticky to the touch) while you are applying it, there is a chance that lap marks can show.

A penetrating-oil gel finish is a new type of finish that makes it easier to apply a high-gloss oil. Normally, penetrating oils are very thin, almost the consistency of water. A gel finish contains ingredients that turn the finish to the consistency of catsup. As the finish is rubbed on, it liquefies and penetrates the wood. Gel finishes are easy to apply, dry fast, and can be built to a high gloss with two or more coats.

To color the wood as you finish it, use a penetrating oil and a stain. Though you can stain the wood before applying a penetrating oil, for the method of application described below it is better to use an oil that has the stain mixed in. If you apply a separate stain first, you will sand *through* the stain. When you use an oil that has the stain mixed in, you will *sand in* the finish. This is preferable.

Another advantage of this type of finish is that the stain used is a dye rather than a pigment. Dye stains reveal all of the wood's character, while a pigmented stain covers up some of the subtle grain characteristics.

Applying a Rubbed Oil Finish

A rubbed oil finish is easy to apply, but like any product that contains solvents and oils, there are certain precautions that should be observed. First, work in a well-ventilated area. The fumes from a penetrating oil are usually not as strong as those from other products containing solvents, but you still need to protect yourself against heavy concentrations of the fumes.

If there isn't adequate ventilation, then use a mask designed to filtre out solvent fumes. Wear plastic gloves to protect your hands from the solvents. Repeated exposure to solvents can cause chapping, skin rashes, and cracks to develop. Dispose of rags used to apply an oil finish in a water-filled metal container with a lid. Oily rags can spontaneously ignite, creating a fire hazard. Don't leave rags in a pile in the work area; always dispose of them after each work session.

Surface preparation is extremely important when penetrating oil finishes are being used. Refer to Chapter 3 for complete directions on surface preparation. Sand the wood carefully, removing any roughness with 100-grit sandpaper. Then switch to 150-grit sandpaper and sand the surface again. Keep sanding with progressively finer sandpaper until the surface is extremely smooth. Use 320-grit sandpaper for the final sanding before you apply the finish. Remove all of the sanding dust with a brush or vacuum cleaner, and then wipe the surface with a tack cloth to get the last remaining dust. The project is now ready to receive the first coat of finish.

A penetrating oil can be applied with a rag, a brush, or by spraying. Unlike a surface coating, the method of application doesn't play an important role in how the final finish looks. The way the finish is applied is simply a matter of which method is most convenient for the job at hand.

For most small projects, a rag is the easiest way to apply the finish. (See Illus. 4-3.) For larger projects, a brush is faster. When the work

Illus. 4-3. A rag can be used to wipe the finish onto the project.

has intricate turnings or carvings, spraying the finish will ensure an even application of the finish in all the nooks and crannies. Penetrating oil is available in aerosol spray cans, so spray equipment is not needed.

Applying a Low-Luster Finish

A low-luster finish is what is typically called a Danish oil finish. It is the type often used on Danish modern furniture. Begin by applying a heavy coat of the finish to the wood. Apply it with a rag or with a brush. (See Illus. 4-4.) Let the oil penetrate for a few minutes. If some spots dry, apply more oil so that the entire surface is wet.

The next step consists of sanding in the finish. Use plastic gloves and 400-grit wet-or-dry sandpaper. Cut the sheet of sandpaper into fourths. Fold one section into a pad about 1½ inch square. Put on the plastic gloves and sand the wet surface of the wood with the 400-grit wet-or-dry sandpaper. Sand with the direction of the grain. (See Illus. 4-5.) If the wood starts to dry, add more finish. Sand the surface thoroughly. As you sand, the sanding dust will mix with the fin-

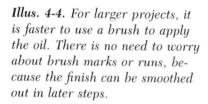

Illus. 4-4. For larger projects, it is faster to use a brush to apply the oil. There is no need to worry about brush marks or runs, because the finish can be smoothed out in later steps.

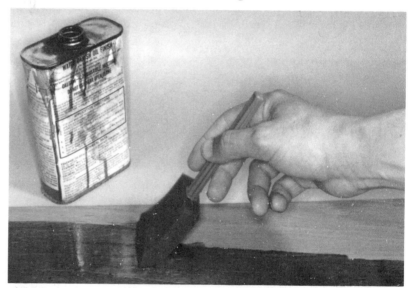

Illus. 4-5. After you have thoroughly wet the surface with oil, sand in the finish using wet-or-dry sandpaper. For a low-luster finish, use 400-grit sandpaper. Sand with the grain. For a higher luster, use 600-grit sandpaper with additional coats.

ish, creating a paste-like mixture. This will fill up the small pores in the wood.

After you have finished sanding, wipe off the surface with a pad of cheesecloth. Wipe in a circular motion to force the mixture of finish and wood dust into the pores of the wood. Then wipe with the grain lightly to remove any swirl marks. (See Illus. 4-6.) It is important that you remove all of the oil that remains on the surface. If some oil remains on the surface, it can get gummy and may not dry properly. Only leave the oil that has soaked into the wood.

It is a good idea to check on the project about an hour after you are done because sometimes oil will seep out of the pores. This is particularly true with open-grained woods like oak and walnut. If you see shiny spots, wipe them off. If you can't remove them with a dry cloth, dampen the cloth with some of the same type of penetrating finish and wipe the area. If you let the spots remain, they will dry and become hard to remove.

Let the finish dry for the time specified on the can, and then apply a second coat. Repeat the procedure above for the second coat and any other coats you apply. Repeat the procedure as many times as you like until the wood has the desired luster. Just remember that if you are using a low-luster oil, you will never create a high gloss; repeated coats will give the finish a soft luster.

For the final coat, apply a small amount of finish with a rag, and then buff the surface with a clean, dry, soft rag. (See Illus. 4-7.)

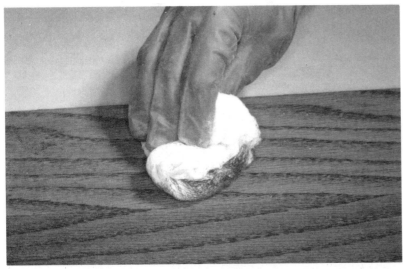

Illus. 4-6. After sanding in the oil, wipe all of the remaining oil off the surface. Any oil that has not soaked into the wood will become a gummy film if it is left on the surface.

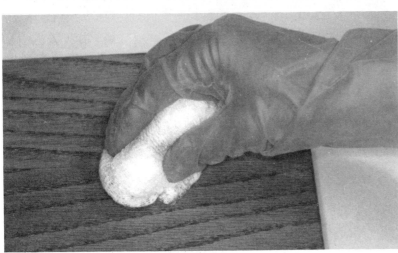

Illus. 4-7. For the final coat, apply a small amount of finish. Don't sand it. Buff it with a clean, dry cloth.

Applying a Medium-Luster Finish

A medium-luster finish is recommended for most projects. It has a satin sheen with enough gloss to give the appearance of a completed finish but without the glare of a high-gloss finish. This is what most people think of as a hand-rubbed finish.

The procedure for applying the first coat of a medium-luster finish is very similar to that used to apply a low-luster finish. Use an oil that is designed to produce a medium luster; most of the penetrating oil products sold are medium-luster finishes. Apply a heavy coat and let the wood absorb as much as it can. Keep the surface wet and sand in the finish with 400-grit sand-paper. Wipe off the remaining finish with a piece of cheesecloth as described above. Be sure to wipe off all the oil that remains on the surface so that it won't get gummy as it dries.

When the first coat is dry, apply a second coat and sand it, but this time with 600-grit sand-paper. Apply as many coats as you like, sanding each lightly with 600-grit wet-or-dry sandpaper.

For the final coat, apply a small amount of oil with a rag and buff it with a clean, dry cloth.

Alternate Method for Rubbing in Oil

The method described above produces the smoothest possible rubbed finish. The following alternate method involves less rubbing and still produces a fine finish. It requires plastic gloves, a synthetic finishing pad or #000 steel wool, and a piece of cheesecloth. This method can be used with low- and medium-luster finishes, but don't use it with high-gloss or gel finishes. The small steel particles that the steel wool sheds can be difficult to remove from the pores of open-grained woods such as oak or walnut, so only use synthetic finishing pads on these woods. (See Illus. 4-8.) For closed-grained hardwoods and softwoods, use either steel wool or synthetic finishing pads.

Illus. 4-8. You can use a synthetic finishing pad or steel wool instead of sandpaper to rub the finish. The synthetic finishing pad is better for open-grained woods, because it won't shed steel particles that can get trapped in the wood's pores.

Begin by pouring some of the finishing oil into a shallow dish or pan. (See Illus. 4-9.) Put on the plastic gloves and dip a synthetic finishing pad or a pad of #000 steel wool into the oil. Wipe the finish onto the wood with the pad. Wipe with wood's grain. (See Illus. 4-10.) Keep dipping the pad into the oil so that you thoroughly wet the surface of the wood. Rub the pad over the wood several times to smooth the wood and work the finish into the surface.

Let the finish soak into the wood for about 10 minutes, and then wipe off the excess with a piece of cheesecloth. (See Illus. 4-11.) If the finish has started to get gummy, moisten the cheesecloth with fresh oil.

Repeat the procedure for each additional coat. Use at least two coats. For the best results, use four or more coats. For the final coat, apply a thin coat of oil with a piece of cheesecloth, and then buff the surface with a dry rag.

Illus. 4-9. Pour some finishing oil in a shallow dish or pan. This makes it easy to dip the steel-wool pad into the oil.

Illus. 4-10. Dip the pad into the oil, and then wipe it on the wood. Wipe with the grain direction. After the entire surface is wet with oil, rub the steel wool over the wood until the surface feels smooth.

Illus. 4-11. Let the oil soak in for about 10 minutes, and then wipe off the excess with a piece of cheesecloth.

Applying a High-Gloss Finish

To create a finish with a high-gloss look, you must use a high-gloss oil. A high-gloss oil is harder to apply, so don't use it for your first project. A certain amount of gloss can be achieved by applying several coats of medium-luster finish, so unless a high-gloss finish is absolutely required, don't use a high-gloss oil.

High-gloss oil doesn't penetrate very deeply into the wood, so if you decide to create a high-gloss finish, begin by applying two coats of low-luster oil. Use the same brand you will use in the high-gloss oil, to ensure compatibility. Sand in the first coat with 400-grit sandpaper, and sand in the second coat with 600-grit sandpaper.

Let the low-luster oil dry completely before applying the high-gloss oil. Don't sand in high-gloss oil; do all of the sanding using low-luster oil. Apply the finish with a ball of cheesecloth. Make the ball by wadding up some cheesecloth and then covering the outside of the cheesecloth with another piece. Tie a piece of string or a garbage-bag tie around the loose ends of the outer cloth to prevent the ball from coming apart. (See Illus. 4-12.)

Completely soak the ball with oil. Hold the ball in the palm of your hand and rub it lightly over the wood surface in long, straight strokes along the grain of the wood. (See Illus. 4-13.) Overlap each stroke slightly so that there are no gaps on the surface. As soon as the ball begins to dry, apply more oil to it. If the surface looks uneven, wipe it again with the cheesecloth ball slightly moistened with finish, but don't let the finish get gummy before you do this or the pad will stick and make a mark. If there is a mark on the finish or you are dissatisfied with it, wipe the finish off with another piece of cheesecloth and start over. You may have to wet the cloth with more finish to loosen a coat that has started to dry on the surface. When you are satisfied with the results, let the finish dry thoroughly before applying another coat.

Illus. 4-12. A ball of cheesecloth makes a good applicator for high-gloss oil. Make the ball by wadding up some cheesecloth, and then wrapping another piece around the outside. Use string or a garbage-bag tie to secure the loose ends.

Illus. 4-13. To apply a high-gloss oil, thoroughly soak the ball with oil, and then hold the ball in the palm of your hand with the tied part up. Wipe the oil on with long, straight strokes with the grain of the wood. Overlap each stroke slightly as you progress across the board.

You can apply as many coats as desired, but each coat will become slightly more difficult to get even, and it will become increasing more difficult to avoid lap marks. The more coats that are applied, the higher the gloss will be.

Applying a Gel Finish

Gel finishes are designed for easy application. They are best for small projects, because they are applied with a rag. Most pieces of furniture are small enough to be finished efficiently with a gel finish. Very large pieces are easier to finish with a traditional oil applied with a brush.

Usually, a gel finish is not sanded in. To prepare the wood, sand it as described in Chapter 3. Use 320-grit sandpaper for the final sanding before applying the finish. Don't sand the bare wood with finer sandpaper. Finer sandpaper will polish the surface, making it more difficult for the finish to soak into the wood.

Squeeze the finish from the bottle onto a clean, lint-free cloth. (See Illus. 4-14.) The type

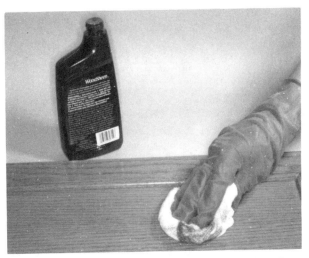

Illus. 4-15. Apply the gel finish by wiping it on the wood with long, even strokes. After you have covered a section, wipe over it again to even out the coating.

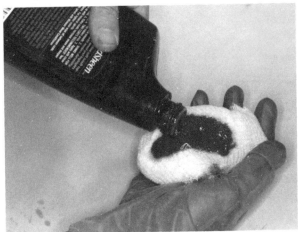

Illus. 4-14. A gel finish is the consistency of catsup when squeezed from the container, but soon liquefies when rubbed on the wood.

sold at paint stores as a staining cloth is effective, but a household rag will also work as long as it doesn't leave lint in the finish.

Apply the finish to the wood by wiping it on with long, straight strokes. Add more finish to the cloth as needed. When you have applied the finish to a small section, wipe it in the direction of the wood's grain to even it out. (See Illus. 4-15.) To create a low-luster finish, wipe off most of the finish that remains on the surface with a clean cloth. For more luster, leave the finish on the surface and let it dry. Additional coats will

add to the luster. It is possible to achieve a high gloss with about three coats.

It isn't necessary to sand between coats, but if there are rough areas, sand them with 400-grit wet-or-dry sandpaper or a synthetic finishing pad. You can use the finishing pad dry. To prevent the sandpaper from clogging, apply a small amount of the gel finish to the sandpaper to act as a lubricant. Wipe off the excess finish immediately after sanding.

Waxing a Rubbed Oil Finish

After any penetrating finish has dried, you can wax it to bring out more luster. For the initial coat of wax, use a paste or liquid wax made specifically for use with penetrating finishes. If the color of the finish is dark, use a wax that is tinted dark brown. If a light wax is used on a dark finish, the wax that builds up in the pores of the wood will turn white and have an undesirable look.

Apply the wax with a soft cloth, rubbing it in with a circular motion. (See Illus. 4-16.) Let it dry as specified on the can, and then wipe it off with a soft cloth. Repeat this step as many times as desired until you are satisfied with the way the finish looks. After the initial waxing, use ordinary furniture wax or lemon oil to maintain the finish.

Repairing a Damaged Rubbed Oil Finish

One of the advantages of a rubbed oil finish is that it can be repaired any time after it has been applied to the wood, and the repaired section will blend in perfectly with the original finish.

Whether the damage is a scratch, a gouge, or a water mark, the repair procedure is the same. Save some of the original oil to use in making repairs, especially if it is an oil that contains a stain. But even if you don't have some of the original oil, you can usually find some that will match. If a clear oil was used originally, simply match the amount of gloss that the original had.

Begin by wetting a pad of 400-grit wet-or-dry sandpaper with oil. Sand the damaged area until the damage has been removed. (See Illus. 4-17.) Add oil as necessary to keep the sandpaper wet.

Now, wipe off the surface and let it dry. If the luster matches the rest of the project after the oil is dry, then you are done. If the repaired area looks dull compared to the rest of the project, sand the area again with a pad of 600-grit sandpaper moistened with the oil. You can add more luster by applying additional coats with a rag and buffing them. Finally, wax the repair and the surrounding area.

Illus. 4-16. For a soft luster and added protection, apply wax after the oil finish is dry. Use a wax that has been tinted to match the finish. Apply it with a rag. Let it dry, and then wipe it off with a soft cloth.

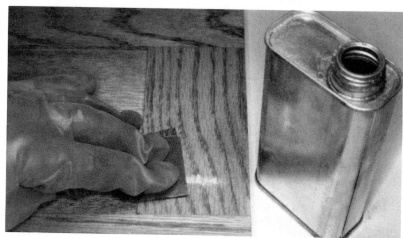

Illus. 4-17. If the oil finish is later damaged, you can easily repair it and restore it to its original beauty. Use the same type of oil as was originally used. Apply oil to the damaged area and sand the area until it is smooth. Apply additional oil, as necessary, to keep the sandpaper wet.

Oil Finishes for Food-Preparation Surfaces

Some types of oil finish may contain material that could be toxic if swallowed. If you are finishing a surface that will come into contact with food, be sure to use an oil that is labelled "Non-Toxic When Dry." A special product called salad-bowl or butcher-block oil is specifically recommended for use on food-preparation areas such as butcher blocks and cutting boards. (See Illus. 4-18.) The procedure for applying butcher-block oil is the same as for any low-luster oil. You can sand in the finish if desired, but since a butcher block will get scratches and cuts during its use, a super-smooth finish is not needed. Usually all that is needed is to apply the finish with a rag and then wipe it off. (See Illus. 4-19.)

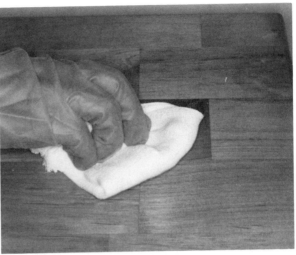

Illus. 4-19. Since food-preparation surfaces will get many nicks and scratches in use, a low-luster finish is best, because it won't highlight the damage as much. There is no need to sand in the finish; just wipe it on, let it soak in, and then wipe off the excess.

Illus. 4-18. An oil finish is excellent for butcher blocks and other food-preparation items, but be sure to use an oil that is recommended for use on food-preparation surfaces.

Exterior Penetrating Finishes

Penetrating finishes are excellent for use on exterior furniture, decks, and railings. (See Illus. 4-20.) The type of finish described above is intended for interior use only. When buying a penetrating finish for exterior use, make sure that you select an exterior penetrating oil.

Try to use a penetrating oil for all exterior projects. If you use a surface coating such as paint or varnish, it will eventually blister and peel. Penetrating finishes withstand the rigors of exterior use better, and when they have become weathered, it is easy to recoat them because they have not blistered or cracked.

Exterior penetrating finishes are often called water-repellent wood preservatives or exterior stains. When you want to highlight the original color of the wood, use a clear, water-repellent finish. To change the color of the wood while revealing its grain, use a transparent or semi-transparent exterior stain. If you want to completely hide the grain of the wood and give the finish the appearance of paint, use a solid-color stain. Solid-color stains should only be used on vertical surfaces such as exterior siding. They are not meant for horizontal surfaces like those found on tables or decks.

Exterior penetrating finishes must be brushed into the wood for the best results. Though they can be applied with spray equipment, you will still have to brush over the surface to work the finish into the wood. For exterior furniture, apply the finish with a brush and let it soak in for 30 minutes. Then wipe off the excess with a rag. For decks, railings, and rough wood, brush on the finish and work it in by brushing back and forth several times. There is no need to wipe it off.

Illus. 4-20. Penetrating oils that are specifically made for exterior use can be used to finish outdoor furniture, decks, and deck railings. They are better than varnish for exterior use, because they will never blister or peel.

Chapter 5
STAINS AND FILLERS

Stains are used to color wood. All wood has a natural color that can be enhanced when a clear finish is applied. When you want to change the color of the wood, use a stain. (See Illus. 5-1.) Fillers are used to fill up the pores of open-grained wood. Woods such as oak, walnut, and mahogany have prominent pores that will show through as a texture on the surface of the top coat. This can be desirable when you use a satin finish and want to highlight some wood texture, but if a smooth surface is desired, you must fill the grain before applying a top coat.

Illus. 5-1. *Stains are used to change or even out the natural color of the wood.*

Types of Stain

Stains are classified by the type of colorant and vehicle used. (The vehicle is the liquid part of the stain.) Colorants can be either pigments or dyes. Dyes soak into the wood, while pigments form a thin layer on top of the wood. Each has certain advantages. Pigmented stains enhance the pattern of the pores, because the pigments build up in the pores. Dye stains enhance other grain features and do not highlight the pore patterns. Pigment stains can be easily detected. A thick layer of solid matter will settle to the bottom of the can of pigmented stain if it is sitting unused for a while. A dye stain remains dissolved, so there isn't much settling.

The vehicle—the liquid part of the stain—must be compatible with the top coat that will be used. The vehicle can be oil-, water-, or solvent-based.

Some stains are called wiping stains. After applying the stain and letting it sit on the wood for a while, wipe it off with a clean rag. You can control the color intensity of the finish by the amount you wipe off. You can also even out the color and eliminate any lap marks while wiping the stain.

Other stains are made to be applied and left on the wood without wiping. These are professional products that require skill to use. Usually, it is best to spray these stains, because brush lap marks are a constant problem.

The novice should use a wiping stain. Some wiping stains contain a gel vehicle. The gel is particularly good for the novice, because it gives him more control over the color intensity and eliminates the possibility of lap marks.

If you are using an oil-based top coat such as polyurethane varnish, use an oil stain. If using water-based varnishes, use a water-based stain. Usually, it is best to use a stain and varnish from the same manufacturer so that you can ensure that they will be compatible. If the stain is incompatible with the top coat, problems can arise later, ranging from discoloration to defects in the top coat.

Choosing a stain color is a matter of personal preference. However, it is important that you test the stain on a sample of the same wood used for the project to determine whether the results will be satisfactory.

Staining Softwood

Softwoods such as pine and fir absorb stains unevenly. This can lead to a blotchy appearance that is dark in some spots and light in others. To ensure an even staining job on softwood, pre-treat the wood with a sealer that will make the wood absorb the stain evenly. A product called wood conditioner may be used for this purpose. Use a wood conditioner that is compatible with the stain you will be using.

After sanding the wood, remove all of the dust, and then apply the wood conditioner. Follow the directions on the container. Usually all you have to do is brush an even coat of the conditioner over the entire surface and let it dry. (See Illus. 5-2.)

Next, apply the stain to a small area of the project. Choose logical stopping places. For example, stain the top of a project, then one side, then the other side, etc. Don't apply the stain to the whole project at once, because you won't be able to wipe it all off before some of it has begun

to dry. (See Illus. 5-3.) The result will be some sections that are darker than others.

If the stain is a liquid, apply it with a brush. A disposable foam brush works well. (See Illus. 5-4.) Apply gel stains with a rag. Let the stain soak into the wood before wiping it.

Sanding in the stain is an effective way to apply it. It helps drive the stain into the wood and smooths out any roughness caused by grain-raising. When you apply a liquid to the surface of wood, some of the fibres will stand up. This creates some roughness. This is more of a problem with water-based stains.

Use 320-grit wet-or-dry sandpaper and plastic gloves to sand in the stain. Fold a piece of the sandpaper into a small pad. Put on the gloves and sand the surface of the board while it is wet with the stain. (See Illus. 5-5.) You'll be able to feel the raised grain while sanding over it. It will make the sandpaper drag. If the stain starts to dry as you are sanding, add slightly more stain. When the sandpaper glides smoothly over the surface, you are done.

A finishing pad can also be used to sand in the finish. The pad acts like a sponge, so you can use it to wipe on the stain and sand it in in a single step. (See Illus. 5-6.)

Illus. 5-2. Softwoods like pine and fir can appear blotchy when stain is applied. To even out the color, apply a wood conditioner before applying the stain.

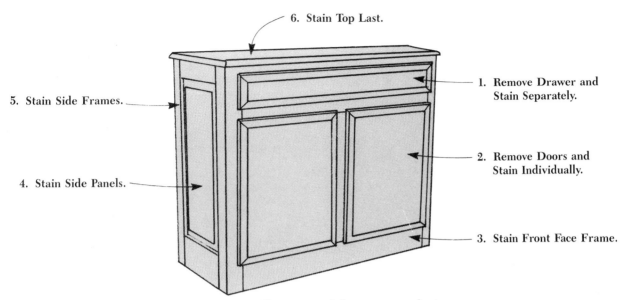

6. Stain Top Last.

1. Remove Drawer and
   Stain Separately.

5. Stain Side Frames.

2. Remove Doors and
   Stain Individually.

4. Stain Side Panels.

3. Stain Front Face Frame.

Illus. 5-3. It is best to apply the stain to small sections of the project and wipe it before it dries. The drawing shows one way the stain could be applied to this project.

Illus. 5-4. Apply the stain with a brush. A disposable foam brush works well for applying stain.

Illus. 5-5. Sand in the stain while it is wet. Use 320-grit wet-or-dry sandpaper. Sand with the grain of the wood. This step is particularly important if you are using a water-based product, because it will remove any raised grain.

Illus. 5-6. A synthetic finishing pad can be used to apply the stain and sand it in in a single step. Wet the pad with stain and wipe it on in a long, straight stroke with the grain of the wood. Then rub the pad over the wood until all of the raised grain has been removed.

Now, use a clean, dry, lint-free cloth to wipe the stain. Staining cloths are available at stores that sell finishing supplies. These cloths work well and are inexpensive. Unlike household rags, they don't leave any lint on the surface. A small piece of lint will make an ugly bump in a coat of varnish.

Wipe the stain on following the grain of the wood. (See Illus. 5-7.) How much you wipe on

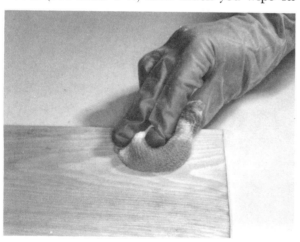

Illus. 5-7. Let the stain soak into the wood for a while, and then wipe it off with a rag. You can control the intensity of the color to some degree by the amount of stain you wipe off.

depends on the color intensity desired. Some boards naturally stain darker than others. You can even out these variations as you wipe by leaving more stain on the lighter boards.

After you have stained the entire project, let the stain dry for the amount of time specified on the container before applying the top coats. If the stain isn't dark enough, apply a second coat.

Staining and Filling Hardwood

Stains can be applied much more evenly to hardwoods, such as birch, oak, mahogany, and walnut, than to softwoods, so a wood conditioner is usually not needed. Begin by applying the stain to a small section with a brush. Sand in the stain as described in the section above, and then wipe it off.

Many hardwoods are open-grained, which means that there are visible pores on the surface of the wood. (See Illus. 5-8.) At this point, decide whether to fill the grain or not. If a high-gloss finish is desired, fill the grain. If you will be using a satin top coat, determining whether to fill

Illus. 5-8. Many popular hardwoods are open-grained. The tiny, exposed pores on this piece of oak give the surface a texture that can be very attractive. In some cases, it is desirable to fill the grain to produce a smooth surface.

the grain is simply a matter of personal preference. If the project has many intricate carvings, turnings, or cutouts, don't fill the grain. It can be very difficult to wipe the excess filler from these areas, and the accumulated filler will ruin the appearance of the project. Filler is best suited for projects with flat surfaces.

Use paste wood filler to fill the grain. Don't confuse this product with wood putty, which is used to fill nail holes and defects in a board. Paste wood filler is a product specifically designed to fill the small pores on the wood surface.

Make sure that the paste wood filler is compatible with the other finishing products you are using. Use stain, paste filler, and varnish that are all made by the same company. Read the label of the paste filler before buying the other products, and use the stain and varnish recommended on the label.

Some water-based varnish is not compatible with oil-based paste wood filler. If you apply an incompatible top coat over paste wood filler, the finish may peel, blister or discolor. These effects may take a while to show up, so even if the finish looks good in a test sample, problems could arise later. Some companies make a water-based filler that is compatible with their other water-based finishing products.

Paste wood filler is available in several colors. Choose a color that is slightly darker than the stain you used. If the stain and the filler are compatible, you can use natural filler and mix some stain with it to get the right color. Universal tinting colors can also be used to color the filler.

Oil-based filler usually comes in a concentrated form that must be thinned before use. Follow the directions on the can for thinning. Mixing the stain with the filler may be all that's needed to thin the filler. Otherwise, use the type of thinner specified on the container. Add thinner and mix until the filler is the consistency of heavy paint. (See Illus. 5-9.) If you want to tint the filler with universal tinting colors, add a small amount after the filler has been thinned. Water-based filler may not need thinning. Be sure to read the directions.

Apply the filler to a small section of the project

Illus. 5-9. Oil-based paste wood filler must be thinned before use. Use the type of thinner and proportions recommended on the can. Some water-based fillers can be applied without being thinned.

with a brush. Foam brushes don't work well in this case. Use a brush with bristles. (See Illus. 5-10.) Work the filler into the wood by brushing back and forth. Let the filler dry a few minutes.

Illus. 5-10. Apply the filler with a brush. A traditional bristle brush works best for this application, because it will hold more of the filling material, which will also work itself into the pores better than it would with a foam brush.

Refer to the directions on the can for the exact time. You can usually tell when it is dry. It will have lost the glossy appearance it had when you applied it and will look very dull.

Now, use a piece of cheesecloth or burlap to wipe the filler off the wood. (See Illus. 5-11.) As you wipe it off, watch to make sure that the filler remains in the open pores. If it is being wiped out of the pores, work it back in by rubbing the rag across the grain of the wood. Finish by wiping the surface with a clean cloth along the wood's grain. Be sure to remove all of the filler from the surface. It should only remain in the pores. Filler left on the surface can cause roughness in the top coats.

Let the filler dry completely before proceeding with the top coats. If the surface feels gritty after the filler is dry, you didn't wipe off all of the excess. Wipe the surface with a clean piece of cheesecloth to remove the grit. If that doesn't produce a smooth-feeling surface, lightly rub the surface with a synthetic finishing pad. (See Illus. 5-12.) You can also use #000 steel wool, if you are not using a water-based finish. (Don't use steel wool if you are using water-based products.) Be careful not to rub through the stain.

 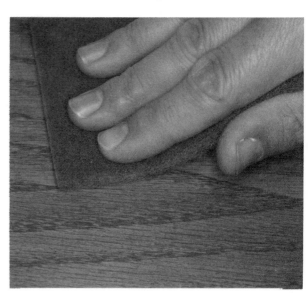

Illus. 5-11 (above left). *Let the filler soak into the wood as specified on the container, and then wipe it off with a piece of burlap or cheesecloth.* ***Illus. 5-12 (above right).*** *After the filler is dry, remove any residue left on the surface by rubbing it with a synthetic finishing pad.*

Chapter 6

VARNISHES

Varnish is a surface coat. It will soak into the surface slightly, but most of the finish remains on the surface of the board. This surface coating repels water and protects the wood surface from dirt and damage. There are other types of clear surface coating. Some of these surface coatings are covered in the next chapter. Varnish is the easiest to apply and is very durable. The novice should use a varnish for most projects that require a surface coating. (See Illus. 6-1.)

Illus. 6-1. Varnish is a surface coating that protects the wood from dirt and abrasion and repels water.

Types of Varnish

There are many types of varnish. Traditional varnish is made from natural resins and oils. Modern varnishes use synthetic resins. Polyurethane is the most widely used synthetic resin varnish. Varnish is available in satin or high gloss.

Many varnishes still have solvents with harmful fumes, but more and more manufacturers are producing water-based varnishes. If you tried a water-based varnish several years ago and were disappointed with the results, don't let that prevent you from trying the new water-based varnishes. Many of the new varnishes perform as well or better than oil-based varnishes. (See Illus. 6-2.) In fact, some are so durable that they are the recommended finish for the hardwood floors of bowling lanes. Once a water-based varnish is dry, it is resistant to water, detergents, and alcohol.

Water-based varnishes are much more pleasant to work with than oil-based varnishes. There are less fumes, and the varnish can be cleaned up with water while wet. Even though these products are very safe, you should still wear plastic gloves and work near an open window when using them.

Illus. 6-2. Modern water-based varnishes are easy to apply and are durable. The results can be as good or better than those achieved with the older, oil-based varnishes. A foam brush makes a good applicator for water-based varnishes.

Applying Water-Based Varnish

Before applying the varnish, make sure that all of the wood preparation is done. If you stain the wood, use a water-based stain that is compatible with the brand of varnish being used. If you sand in the stain as recommended in Chapter 5, then proceed with the varnish application. If you are applying varnish to unstained wood, you will have to raise the wood's grain and sand the wood again before applying the varnish.

Use compatible fillers and varnishes to avoid problems in the finish coat. Do not use oil-based paste wood filler with water-based varnish, unless the manufacturer specifically states in the directions that the varnish is compatible with oil-based paste wood filler. If you want to use an oil-based paste wood filler, use an oil-based varnish.

Some companies make a water-based filler that is compatible with their water-based varnish.

Any water-based product will cause some grain to rise. With many of the new varnishes, the amount of grain-raising has been reduced, but there will still be some. Grain-raising occurs when the wood fibres on the surface of the board absorb water. This causes them to stand up. Even after they dry, they still are raised above the surface. This produces a rough texture in the varnish. Sanding in a water-based stain before varnishing will prevent the grain from rising in the varnish coat.

When no stain is used, wet-sanding the wood before applying the varnish can prevent problems with raised grain. Doing this requires a sponge, a container of water, and 320-grit wet-or-dry sandpaper. Work on one small section at a time. Wet the sponge, and then wring out most of the water. Don't soak the wood surface, just dampen it. Wipe the wet sponge over the wood. (See Illus. 6-3.) Then fold the 320-grit wet-or-dry sandpaper into a small pad. Dip it in the water to wet it.

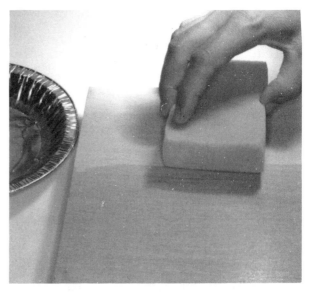

Illus. 6-3. If you used a water-based stain and sanded it as recommended in Chapter 5, then you can apply the varnish without any additional preparation. Before applying water-based varnish to bare wood, raise the grain and sand it smooth. Use a damp sponge to wet the board.

Now, sand the surface of the wood, working with the grain direction. (See Illus. 6-4.) If the sandpaper starts to dry out, dip it into the water again. When the surface feels smooth, wipe it dry with a rag. (See Illus. 6-5.) Let the wood dry overnight, and then sand it again lightly with 320-grit sandpaper. (See Illus. 6-6.) By this procedure, you raise the grain of the wood and sand off the raised fibres before applying the varnish. When you apply the varnish, the fibres that

Illus. 6-6. *When the wood is completely dry, lightly sand it with 320-grit sandpaper.*

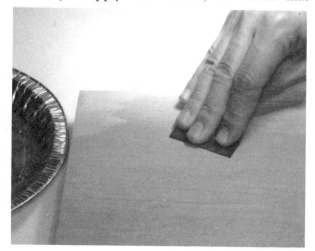

Illus. 6-4. *Use 320-grit wet-or-dry sandpaper to wet-sand the wood. This will remove the raised grain.*

would have risen are gone, so the finish is smoother.

Synthetic finishing pads can also be used to remove raised grain. Dip the pad into water and ring it out until it is just damp. Rub the pad over the wood, adding more water as necessary to wet the surface of the wood. When the wood is wet, rub the pad over the surface several times until it feels as if all of the rough raised grain has been removed. (See Illus. 6-7.) Let the wood dry, and

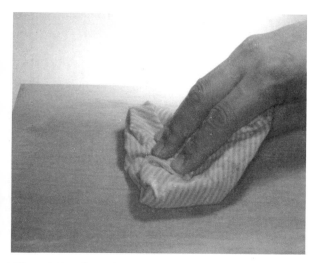

Illus. 6-5. *When the surface feels smooth, wipe it dry with a rag. Too much water left on the wood for a long time can cause problems. Be particularly careful with plywood or veneer, because the water can soften the glue and cause delamination.*

Illus. 6-7. *A synthetic finishing pad can be used instead of sandpaper to raise the grain. Dip the pad in water, and then wipe it over the wood's surface. Keep rubbing the surface until the raised grain has been removed.*

then wipe the surface again with a dry finishing pad.

When applying varnish, work in a clean, dust-free area. Varnish can remain tacky (sticky to the touch) for several hours. Each particle of dust that lands on the project during that time will create a small bump on the surface. This is an excellent reason to use a fast-drying varnish. The more quickly the varnish becomes tack-free, the less chance there is that dust will get on the surface.

Remove all dust from the project before applying the varnish. Use a vacuum with a brush attachment (see Illus. 6-8) or a bristle brush to remove most of the dust, and then wipe the surface with a tack cloth to remove the last remaining dust. (See Illus. 6-9.)

Read and follow the directions on the varnish container carefully. Each product has some different characteristics, so the directions in this chapter can only be general ones. When you open the can of varnish, it may look more like white paint than clear varnish. Don't be concerned; water-based varnish dries crystal-clear. In fact, it is so clear that some manufacturers offer an amber additive to give the finish the look of traditional varnish, which has an amber tint. In most cases, this additive is not necessary. The

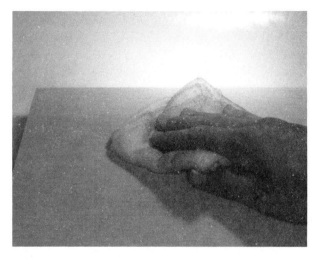

Illus. 6-9. Immediately before applying the varnish, wipe the entire project with a tack cloth to remove the last traces of dust.

exceptional clarity of water-based varnish is an advantage, because it won't change the color of the wood or stain.

Before using the varnish, gently stir it with a paint-stirring stick. (See Illus. 6-10.) Don't shake the can or use a drill-mounted paint stirrer, because this creates a lot of bubbles. The bubbles will cling to the brush and flow onto the surface of the wood as you apply the varnish. These bubbles are difficult to remove. If you let the varnish

Illus. 6-8. It is very important that you remove all of the dust from the wood before applying varnish. Small dust particles will cause rough bumps on the finished surface of the varnish. Begin by brushing or vacuuming the dust from the project.

Illus. 6-10. The varnish must be stirred before use. Stir gently so that you won't create many bubbles. Note that this water-based varnish appears to be opaque-white in the can. It will dry to a crystal-clear color when applied to the wood.

dry with bubbles on it, the result will be a rough crater wherever there was a bubble.

The best way to handle the problem of bubbles is to avoid creating bubbles in the first place. Stir the varnish effectively with a stick and a slow stirring motion. This will take longer than other methods, but will prevent bubbles from forming.

Now, apply the varnish. Work on one section of the project at a time. Some types of varnish can be applied with a rag, while others must be applied by brush. In either case, apply a thin coat. Build up the thickness of the coating by applying additional coats.

If you are using the type of varnish that can be applied with a rag, use a lint-free cloth. Fold the cloth into a pad that will fit comfortably into your hand. Wear plastic gloves to protect your hands and make cleanup easier. Moisten the pad with varnish. Wipe the pad over the wood in a long, straight stroke with the grain. Work fast, to cover the surface.

Overlap each stroke slightly. Add varnish to the pad as it dries out. When the surface has been covered, wring out the pad and wipe it lightly over the entire surface to even out the finish. (See Illus. 6-11.) Let the finish dry undisturbed. If you try to smooth it out after it becomes tacky, the surface will become rough.

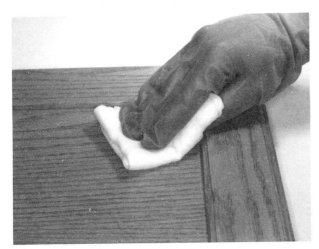

Illus. 6-11. Some water-based varnishes are made to be wiped on with a rag. This is a very easy way to create a smooth, even top coat. Be sure to follow all of the manufacturer's recommendations when applying varnish.

To brush on varnish, use a 2½-inch-wide brush for most projects. A foam brush does a better job of applying varnishes than a bristle brush. Dip the brush into the varnish. Don't immerse the brush up to its handle; stop when the bristles are about halfway into the varnish. (See Illus. 6-12.) Gently wipe any excess varnish off on the lip of the can as you withdraw the brush.

Illus. 6-12. Use a foam brush to brush on water-based varnish. Dip the brush into the can until the bristles are immersed halfway; then remove the brush and gently wipe off the excess on the lip of the can.

Apply the varnish in long, straight strokes in the direction of the grain of the wood. (See Illus. 6-13.) Work quickly on a small section at a time. Once you have covered the section, go over it again lightly with the brush, but don't add any more varnish. This will flatten the surface and even out any thick or thin spots.

For large, flat areas such as a tabletop, use a pad applicator. This is a finishing tool that resembles a sponge mop with a piece of short-napped carpet attached to it. A pad applicator can be

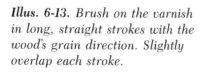

Illus. 6-13. Brush on the varnish in long, straight strokes with the wood's grain direction. Slightly overlap each stroke.

used to cover a large area rapidly with a minimum of brush marks.

To use a pad applicator, pour some of the varnish into a roller tray. Dip the applicator into the varnish, and then squeeze it against the sloped part of the tray to remove the excess. Place the pad on the work and move it in a steady stroke from one end to the other. (See Illus. 6-14.) Apply moderate downward pressure to the pad and tilt it slightly so that it is more compressed at the back. This will spread out the varnish in a very thin, smooth coat. The pad applicator will hold enough varnish for the entire length of the surface, so you do not have to stop to add more varnish. This produces a very smooth coat of varnish.

Dip the pad into the varnish again for the next stroke. Overlap the strokes about ½ inch. Since most water-based varnishes begin to dry soon after application, try to get a smooth coat with the initial application. If you go back to try to smooth out irregularities, the varnish may have begun to dry. Brushing over it a second time will roughen it instead of smoothing it out. If you must go over the areas a second time, do it immediately after making the first stroke. Don't wait until the entire surface is covered.

Most water-based varnishes have to be sanded between coats. The finish won't adhere to the surface well if you don't remove the gloss by sanding it. Sanding also removes any raised grain

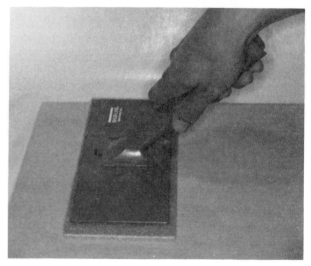

Illus. 6-14. The pad applicator is a very good tool for applying varnish to large, flat areas. It will create a smooth, flat coat that does not have brush marks.

or dust nibs. Use 320-grit sandpaper or a synthetic finishing pad for sanding between coats. Do not use steel wool. Steel wool can leave behind small steel fibres that will react with the next coat of varnish to leave a discolored spot. Don't use sandpaper that has an anti-clogging compound. This compound can react with the finish and cause small craters called fisheyes in the finish. Sandpaper that has this anti-clogging compound is usually white or grey. Untreated sandpaper will be almost black.

Make sure that the finish is completely dry before you begin to sand. If it is still wet, sanding it will cause it to ball up and leave large streaks on the surface.

A synthetic finishing pad is the easiest way to prepare the surface for the next coat. Rub the pad over the varnish in long, straight strokes with the direction of the grain. (See Illus. 6-15.) Stop when the surface is uniformly dull. Don't rub too hard or you may cut completely through the varnish.

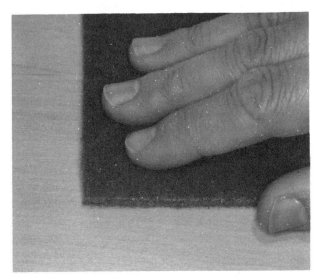

Illus. 6-15. Many water-based varnish manufacturers recommend sanding between coats to smooth out rough spots and to provide adequate adhesion between the coats. A synthetic finishing pad can be used to perform this operation. The finishing pad is flexible, so it will conform to surface irregularities, and it won't get clogged up with residue from the varnish. Rub the pad in long, straight strokes with the grain direction.

If you are going to use sandpaper, use a sanding block with a soft backing. (See Illus. 6-16.) There are two reasons for using a flexible sanding block. First, it prevents the sandpaper from cutting into the finish. Second, the soft backing allows the sandpaper to follow small irregularities in the surface so that the entire surface gets sanded evenly.

The purpose of sanding between coats is to create a uniformly dull surface and to level off

Illus. 6-16. If you use sandpaper between coats of varnish, use a padded sanding block so that the sandpaper will conform to any dips or bumps in the surface. At this stage in the process, the objective is not to flatten the surface; that should have been accomplished during the initial surface preparation. If you use an unpadded sanding block, you run the risk of sanding through to bare wood on high spots and leaving low spots unsanded.

any raised grain or dust nibs. Once you have achieved this, stop sanding; there is no need to remove a lot of material.

Sand along the grain of the wood and use light pressure on the sanding block. When you are done sanding, wipe away the dust with a tack cloth. (See Illus. 6-17.)

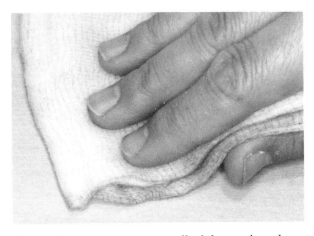

Illus. 6-17. You must remove all of the sanding dust produced as you sand between the coats. Immediately before applying the next coat, wipe the surface with a tack cloth.

Applying Oil-Based Varnish

Although water-based varnishes are quickly becoming more popular than oil-based varnishes, there are still some situations where an oil-based varnish is needed. One such situation occurs if you plan on rubbing the varnish as described in Chapter 8. For the best results with a rubbed finish, use a varnish made with natural resins and oils. This type of varnish will usually be labelled a rubbing varnish. The rubbing process uses fine abrasives to smooth the finish. A rubbing varnish has properties that make it suitable for this process. It must dry hard, yet not so hard that it can't be polished effectively. When the varnish has the correct properties, the fine scratches left by the abrasive can be buffed out with wax and a soft cloth. The buffing process breaks off the sharp peaks between the scratches. If the varnish is too hard, the peaks won't break off. This makes the scratches much more visible. Do not use synthetic varnishes. They are too "hard."

An oil-based varnish is usually also used when an oil-based paste wood filler has been used to fill the pores of an open-grained wood. If you don't plan on rubbing the finish, then an oil-based polyurethane is a good choice.

There is usually no need to raise the grain before applying an oil-based varnish. Just prepare the wood as described in Chapter 3. If staining the wood, use an oil-based stain that is compatible with the varnish you are using.

Stir the varnish with a stirring stick; try to avoid making bubbles. Apply the varnish with a brush, preferably a 2½-inch-wide foam brush. If using a bristle brush, select a high-quality natural-bristle brush.

Follow the manufacturer's recommendation as to how heavy a coat to apply. Some varnishes work best with a thicker application that will form an even coat. However, don't apply a coat that's so thick it begins to sag or run. Generally, you will have fewer problems when applying a coat that is too thin than with one that is too

Illus. 6-18. A foam brush also works well when you are applying an oil-based varnish. Begin by applying the varnish in long, straight strokes with the wood's grain direction. Slightly overlap each stroke.

thick. Apply a coat of varnish with long, even strokes.

The following method works well when working with slow-drying, oil-based varnishes. Begin by applying varnish in long, even strokes with the grain of the wood. (See Illus. 6-18.) Next, brush over the entire surface again along the wood's grain, but don't add any varnish to the brush. (See Illus. 6-19.) The purpose of this step is to even out the coat and spread the varnish uniformly over the surface.

The final step is called tipping-off. Hold the

Illus. 6-19. Brush out the varnish by going over the surface again with the brush, but don't add any more varnish. This will even out the application by spreading varnish from thick areas into other sections that received less varnish.

brush straight up and down so that just the tip touches the surface. Brush lightly, along the wood's grain, over the entire surface. (See Illus. 6-20.)

Illus. 6-20. The tipping-off process smooths out any remaining brush marks. Hold the brush so that it's almost vertical. Lightly touch the tip of the brush to the surface and drag it across the board in long strokes that run from one edge to the other with the grain.

On large, flat surfaces like tabletops, it is especially important to apply a uniform coat of varnish. The pad-applicator method described above also works well with oil-based varnish. Since oil-based varnish dries more slowly than water-based varnish, after you have covered the entire surface, you can go over it again with the pad to smooth out the finish. Don't apply any more varnish to the pad for this operation. Let the varnish dry completely before proceeding with the next step. It may take several days for the varnish to completely harden.

When the first coat is dry, prepare it for the next coat by rubbing the surface with a synthetic finishing pad. (See Illus. 6-21.) Since this is not a water-based finish, you can also use #000 steel wool, but be sure to remove all of the steel particles before applying the next coat. You can also use 220-grit sandpaper. Use a rubber sanding block. Wipe the dust off with a tack cloth.

Illus. 6-21. When the first coat is dry, smooth it by rubbing a synthetic finishing pad over the surface.

Apply the second coat using the same technique as described above. You can use a finishing pad between all varnish coats, but for the smoothest possible finish, wet-sand between coats after the second coat.

After the second coat is dry, wet-sand it using 400-grit wet-or-dry sandpaper and a rubber sanding block. Fill a flat pan with water and dip the sandpaper into the water. Sand with the wood's grain, dipping the sandpaper into the water frequently. (See Illus. 6-22.) Occasionally, wipe the surface dry with a clean cloth to check your progress. When the surface is uniformly dull, you are done. Areas that are shiny have to be sanded more.

Don't sand so hard that you cut through the varnish to the wood below. If you can't get some areas dull with a reasonable amount of sanding, use a pad of #0000 steel wool. Steel wool is also good for reaching into areas that can't be reached with a sanding block. (See Illus. 6-23.) Rub the steel wool over the shiny spot until it is dull. Dry the surface completely with a clean cloth, and then remove any remaining dust with a tack cloth. (See Illus. 6-24.)

If you are applying a satin polyurethane, two coats may be sufficient. For a high-gloss polyurethane, use at least three coats. When using rubbing varnish, apply four coats.

Illus. 6-22. The second coat and all later coats except the final coat should be wet-sanded with 400-grit wet-or-dry sandpaper.

Illus. 6-23. In areas that can't be reached with a sanding block, use #0000 steel wool to smooth the varnish.

Illus. 6-24. Dry the project thoroughly with a clean cloth. Try to minimize the amount of time that water remains on the wood so that it won't soak into crevasses and cause problems.

Varnishing Problems and Solutions

Sags and Drips

Sags and drips occur when the varnish is applied too thickly. If you notice a sag or drip soon after the varnish has been applied, brush it out. Wipe most of the varnish out of the brush and brush lightly over the affected area. The best solution is to avoid sags and drips altogether. This can be accomplished by applying a thin coat in the first place.

Rough Surface

A rough surface is usually caused by raised grain or dust that has settled on the varnish. Once a varnish has a rough surface, there is nothing you can do about it while the varnish is wet. Let the varnish dry, and then sand the surface smooth with 220-grit sandpaper. If the rough surface was caused by raised grain, there won't be any further occurrence. If it was caused by dust, be sure to move to a dust-free location before applying the next coat. Apply another coat of varnish and proceed as usual.

Fisheyes

Fisheyes are small craters in the surface of the dried varnish. They are caused when the varnish doesn't adhere to the surface below those areas. Usually, a foreign substance on the surface is the cause of fisheyes. The anti-clogging compound on some types of sandpaper can also cause fisheyes. Silicone is an ingredient used in some furniture polishes. It can cause severe fisheye problems.

If you notice fisheyes developing while the varnish is wet, brush over the area several times to try to get the varnish to stick. If the varnish is dry before you notice the fisheyes, sand the surface with 220-grit sandpaper. Some manufacturers offer a product that destroys fisheyes. This product can be added to the varnish for the next coat. Manufacturers also sell a special cleaner that will remove silicone. If the fisheyes are caused by silicone, clean the surface with this special cleaner before applying the next coat.

Wrinkles

Wrinkles are caused when a very heavy amount of varnish builds up in one area. As the varnish dries, it wrinkles. To remove wrinkles, scrape the wrinkled section off with a putty knife. Let the underlying varnish dry thoroughly, and then sand the area with 220-grit sandpaper.

Blocking

When a finish remains slightly tacky after it is dry, it has a condition called blocking. This can be a big problem in projects like bookcases and tables, because anything that is placed on the surface will stick to it, leaving a mark when it is removed.

Blocking is usually caused by an inferior-quality varnish. If the finish has blocking, let it dry for several weeks. If it still has blocking after that, then apply a better varnish on top of the previous finish. Test for compatibility by applying the varnish to a small area that isn't noticeable. If the new varnish doesn't lift the previous varnish or show other undesirable properties, apply it to the entire project. Sand the previous finish with 400-grit sandpaper before applying the new varnish. Usually one coat of the new varnish is all that is necessary.

Chapter 7

OTHER TOP COATS

Sometimes a special situation will arise when you need to use a top coat that is slightly more difficult to apply than varnish. (See Illus. 7-1.) These other top coats are usually used by professionals. For complete information on these products, re- fer to the *Wood Finisher's Handbook*. The information in this book is intended for the novice wood finisher. The top coats covered in this chapter are shellac, lacquer, shading lacquer, and varnish stain. Each is described below.

Illus. 7-1. You can use a penetrating-oil finish or a varnish on most projects, but in special situations you may want to use one of the other top coats covered in this chapter. This cabinet is an antique reproduction; for a look of complete authenticity, it is being finished with shellac.

Shellac

Shellac has been used as a finishing material for centuries. Its most common use today is for refinishing antiques and finishing antique reproductions. Shellac is a durable finish that has withstood the test of time on many antiques, but it is susceptible to water damage, and alcohol will dissolve it.

Experienced wood finishers buy shellac in a dry form and mix a fresh batch when needed. The novice should buy liquid shellac.

Shellac has a limited shelf life. There will be an expiration date printed on the can. Be sure to use the shellac before the expiration date. Using outdated shellac can result in a finish that remains tacky and never completely dries.

Alcohol is the solvent in shellac. The amount of solvent in relation to the amount of shellac is referred to as the *cut*. Most liquid shellac comes as a four-pound cut. This means that four pounds of dry shellac are dissolved in one gallon of alcohol. If you need to thin shellac, be sure to use alcohol that is sold specifically for this purpose. If you use the wrong type, problems may arise with the finish.

There are various types of shellac. The two most commonly available are orange and white. Orange shellac retains some of the color of the natural shellac. It has an orange-brown color. This is the type to use if you want to duplicate the finish found on old antiques. White shellac has been processed to remove all of its color. It is completely clear. This is the type to use if you don't want the top coat to alter the color of the wood or the stain previously used.

Shellac can be applied by a process called French polishing. This is the method used by advanced wood finishers. It produces a high-quality, smooth finish. In French polishing, a pad is used to apply the finish. The French polishing process can be difficult to master, so the novice should avoid it. If you are interested in French polishing, refer to the *Wood Finisher's Handbook*.

For beginners, brushing shellac on is the best method of application. Use a high-quality natural-bristle brush. The alcohol solvent will affect synthetic brushes and foam brushes, so they can't be used.

Although shellac can be brushed on directly from the can, better results can be achieved if it is thinned first. Thin it with shellac thinner that can be bought at any store where shellac is sold. Mix two parts thinner to one part shellac (four-pound cut) to get a one-pound-cut shellac. (See Illus. 7-2.) It will take many coats to build up the finish using shellac this thin, but the result will be a very smooth finish.

After you have sanded and stained the wood, apply the first coat of shellac. Use the one-pound cut for the first coat, even if you want to use a heavier cut for later coats. Apply the shellac in long, even strokes with the grain of the wood. Work quickly, because the shellac will begin to dry almost as soon as you apply it. Don't do a lot of brushing over an area, because the shellac will start to dry and you will leave brush marks. Just brush it on and move to the next section. (See Illus. 7-3.)

Let the first coat dry for four hours, and then sand it with 320-grit sandpaper. (See Illus. 7-4.) Just sand enough to remove any roughness. Shellac will clog the sandpaper quickly. Using #000 steel wool (Illus. 7-5) or a synthetic finishing pad instead of sandpaper will eliminate clogging. (See Illus. 7-6.) The next coat of shellac will slightly dissolve the first coat and weld the two coats together, so there is no need to rough up the entire surface for good adhesion.

For the best finish, continue using the one-pound-cut shellac for the rest of the coats. Brush on a coat and let it dry for four hours. Sand it with 320-grit sandpaper or use #000 steel wool or a synthetic finishing pad between coats to remove any roughness; then apply another coat. Keep

Illus. 7-2. Shellac is usually thinned before use. Be sure to use the type of alcohol that is specifically made for use as shellac thinner.

Illus. 7-3. Shellac dries fast, so apply it quickly and don't brush over the area after the initial application. Be sure to use a natural-bristle brush. The alcohol solvent in shellac will destroy foam and synthetic-bristle brushes.

Illus. 7-4. You can sand between coats of shellac to remove rough spots, but this is not necessary for proper adhesion, because the new coat will slightly dissolve the old one and the two coats will meld together.

Illus. 7-5. Steel wool works well for smoothing between coats of shellac. Shellac won't clog steel wool as it does sandpaper.

Illus. 7-6 (right). A synthetic finishing pad can also be used between coats of shellac. It works like steel wool, but it lasts longer, and it doesn't shed steel particles on the project.

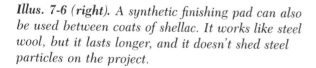

adding coats until you have created the finish you want. This method requires at least five coats.

For a faster finish, apply a one-pound-cut as the first coat, and then use the four-pound-cut directly from the can for the next coat. You can achieve a thick finish in two or three coats with this method, but it is harder to avoid brush marks when using the thicker shellac.

Lacquer

Lacquer is the professional's choice for most finishing jobs, but it can be difficult for the beginner to use. When professionally applied, lacquer is almost always sprayed. Usually the only time a novice would need to use lacquer is to refinish a section of a piece that had been already finished with lacquer. And even in this case, a varnish could be used, because a varnish can be applied over lacquer. Lacquer, however, can never be applied over varnish. Lacquer contains strong solvents that will damage the underlying varnish, creating a rough or wrinkled surface.

If you must apply lacquer, use a special brushing lacquer that dries more slowly than spraying lacquer. Be sure to wear gloves and a respirator and work in a well-ventilated area. The solvents in lacquer are harmful and can cause health problems if you receive a heavy exposure.

Use a natural-bristle brush to apply lacquer. The solvents will dissolve synthetic brushes and foam brushes. Even brushing lacquer dries quickly, so work quickly. Brush on a very thin coat. (See Illus. 7-7.) Don't brush over the same area again, because the lacquer will begin to dry immediately.

After the first coat is dry, sand it with 320-grit sandpaper to remove any roughness. You can also use #000 steel wool or a synthetic finishing pad between coats if you prefer. Be sure to remove all of the sanding dust and steel-wool particles with a tack cloth before applying a second coat. The procedure is much the same as described for shellac. It is best to apply many thin coats. Use sandpaper or steel wool between coats to remove roughness, but don't rough up the surface if it is

Illus. 7-7. Lacquer is a professional product that is usually applied with spray equipment. You can also apply it with a brush, if you use a special brushing lacquer that dries slower than spraying lacquer. Use a natural-bristle brush, because the strong solvent in lacquer will attack foam brushes and synthetic-bristle brushes. Apply lacquer in thin coats. Brush it on quickly, and don't brush over the area again after the lacquer has started to get sticky.

smooth. Each coat welds to the previous one by slightly dissolving the underlying finish.

Lacquer is a very good finish to rub. Refer to Chapter 8 for details.

Shading Lacquer

A shading lacquer has a stain and a lacquer. This saves time because the stain and top coat can be applied in a single operation. This product is frequently used by furniture manufacturers for mass-produced furniture. Shading lacquer is not recommended for beginners. A better job can usually be done by first staining the wood and then applying a clear top coat.

There are some situations where a shading lacquer can be useful. If you are trying to match the finish on factory-made furniture that was finished at the factory with a shading stain, then the only way to get a close match is to use a shading stain. Better results can be achieved if you use the type of shading stain that comes in a spray can. Note how the original finish was applied. Sometimes it is applied with a technique called glazing or shading. This is what gives shading lacquer its name. Shading is achieved by first applying a thin, even coat to the entire surface, and then going back and adding more stain around the edges and on details that you want to emphasize. This can be done easily with a spray can. Just spray extra coats on the shaded areas. The spray will feather out, so the transition from light to dark will be gradual. (See Illus. 7-8.) It is almost impossible to duplicate this effect with a brush.

Varnish Stain

Varnish stain is a varnish mixed with dyes and pigments to add color. As with shading lacquer,

when varnish stain is used time is saved because a separate staining process is eliminated. This product is not suitable for general use, because it is difficult to apply evenly. When you apply stain, you are trying to create an even color; this may involve wiping some sections harder than others. When you are applying a top coat, the objective is to get an even surface; this means that you can't wipe a varnish stain. When the stain and the top coat are being applied in a single step, it is difficult to get an even coat. So, in most cases you should use a separate stain and top coat. If you use a light-colored varnish stain on a wood that stains well, such as oak, then the results are usually acceptable.

There are some instances where a varnish stain works well, as, for example, when some types of antique finish are being duplicated. In this case,

Illus. 7-8. Shading lacquer is a semi-transparent colored lacquer. It can be sprayed on to create shaded effects.

Illus. 7-9. Varnish stain is a colored varnish. It can be used to imitate the look of orange shellac or old varnish that has darkened with age. It can be applied with a foam brush.

first stain the wood as usual, and then use a dark amber–tinted varnish as the top coat. In this instance, a brushed-on polyurethane makes a good choice. The effect is similar to old varnish that has darkened with age. (See Illus. 7-9.) Orange-brown–colored varnish can also be used to simulate the look of orange shellac. This will give the project an antique look and a durable polyurethane varnish.

Varnish stain is also available in spray cans. This product has proven useful for refinishing old radio cases from the 1930s and 1940s. These radio cases were originally sprayed with a similar product at the factory. (See Illus. 7-10.)

apply a small amount of the new varnish to an inconspicuous spot to test its compatibility. If it seems compatible after it is dry, the varnish can be safely applied to the project. Thoroughly clean the old finish by wiping it with a finishing pad moistened with water and TSP or detergent. (TSP—trisodium phosphate—is a product available at most stores that sell paint that can be mixed with water to clean a finish.) (See Illus. 7-11.) Rinse off the cleaner with a wet rag and then wipe the finish with a dry rag.

Illus. 7-10. The type of varnish stain that comes in a spray can is a close approximation of the finish used on some furniture and radio cabinets made in the 1930s and 1940s. You can use this product to restore or refinish these items.

Illus. 7-11. Before applying varnish stain over an existing finish, clean and dull the surface by rubbing it with a synthetic finishing pad dampened with TSP or detergent and water.

Varnish stain can also be used when you would like to darken the color of an existing finish. If the existing finish is in good condition and you simply want to darken the color, this method will work. If the existing finish is damaged, then it is better to strip the finish and begin again.

To apply varnish stain over the old finish, first

Just before applying the varnish, go over the surface with a tack cloth. (See Illus. 7-12.) Brush or spray the varnish stain onto the surface (See Illus. 7-13.) You must create a very even coat, or the color will look darker in the areas that receive a heavier coat. Let the varnish dry and then rub it with a synthetic finishing pad or #000 steel wool.

Illus. 7-12. Remove all dust immediately before applying the varnish. To do this, wipe the surface with a tack cloth.

Illus. 7-13. Varnish stain can be used to darken an existing finish. Brush the varnish on evenly. Any unevenness will show up as a lighter or darker area.

Next, apply a second coat. This coat should be very thin. If adding a second coat of the varnish stain would darken the color too much, use a compatible clear varnish for the second coat. The result will be a darker finish with a less visible grain pattern. This finish will never look as good as if you stripped the old finish and restained the wood, but it can save much work, especially on large projects and interior woodwork.

Chapter 8

METHODS FOR APPLYING RUBBED FINISHES

To create the ultimate silky-smooth finish, you should rub the top coat. A rubbed finish is typically a satin finish that has slightly more gloss than satin varnish. The rubbing process removes any dust or small imperfections, leaving the smoothest possible surface. (See Illus. 8-1.)

Rubbed finishes are usually used on flat surfaces like tabletops. If the project has many intricate carvings, turnings, or nooks and crannies, then it is better to use satin varnish that is not rubbed.

In this chapter, four ways of rubbing a finish are described. The easiest method involves using steel wool. Steel wool smooths and dulls the surface, producing a satin finish. Another fairly easy method involves using wet-or-dry sandpaper. Sandpaper is better at removing small bumps in the finish than steel wool. Rubbing compound is slightly more difficult to use, but the result will be a finish with more gloss. In the final method, two traditional abrasives called pumice and rottenstone are used. This is the most difficult method, but when it is used, it is possible to achieve a high degree of gloss.

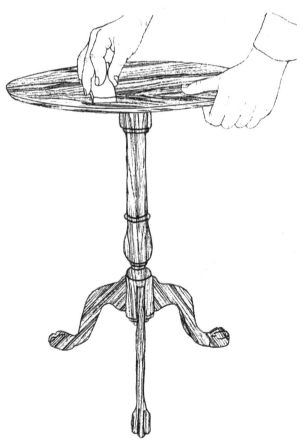

Illus. 8-1. For the ultimate in a silky-smooth finish, rub the top coat. Tabletops often have rubbed finishes, because they are highly visible. A rubbed finish also feels very smooth, which is a plus when used on tabletops or other surfaces that will be touched frequently.

Type of Finish to Use

You must use a top coat that is designed to be rubbed. The best type for the beginner is rubbing varnish. Shellac and lacquer can also be rubbed. So can some types of water-based varnish; they usually work best when the steel-wool method is used. This is one instance when steel wool can be used with a water-based varnish, because the varnish is completely dry and no further coats will be added.

If you want to rub a water-based finish, make a sample board first. Finish the board using the same products you intend to use on the project; then let the board dry for several days. Try rubbing the finish on the sample board. If the results are satisfactory, proceed with the project.

Ordinary polyurethane varnish can be rubbed, but in most cases the results won't be as satisfactory. Polyurethane is so hard it shows the scratches left by the rubbing more prominently. This can lead to a blue haze appearing on the surface when light reflects on it at certain angles. This occurs because the scratches act like tiny prisms breaking up the light. With other finishes, the scratches can be softened by buffing, so they are not as sharply defined. If you rub polyurethane, use a finer abrasive than you would otherwise use.

Finish the project as described in the previous chapters. Apply a rubbing varnish. The method of application is the same as for any gloss varnish. Let the varnish dry completely. Refer to the directions on the can for the exact time. Wait at least a week before rubbing the varnish. Lacquer and shellac dry faster; they can be rubbed the next day.

Steel Wool

Using steel wool is the easiest way to rub a finish. Use the finest grade of steel wool, which is called "four aught" and is written either as #0000 or 4/0. You must lubricate the steel wool during this operation. Several types of wax can be used as a lubricant. A special steel-wool wax that is specifically made for this purpose can be used. So can paste wax or liquid furniture wax. Lemon-oil furniture polish will also work.

Put some wax on the steel wool before you begin rubbing. (See Illus. 8-2.) Now, place the steel-wool pad on the work and make long strokes with the direction of the grain. (See Illus. 8-3.) Rub the entire surface uniformly. Occasionally wipe off the wax and examine the surface. If shiny areas still remain, go over them individually with the steel wool and wax.

Illus. 8-2. Use wax to lubricate the steel wool when rubbing a finish.

Illus. 8-3. Rub the steel wool in long, straight strokes with the grain. Cross-grain strokes or swirling strokes are undesirable, because they will become highly visible when the light strikes the surface at certain angles.

When all of the shiny spots have been eliminated and the surface is smooth and has a uniform satin finish, stop rubbing. Remove most of the wax with a clean, dry cloth. Let the wax dry awhile, and then buff the surface to the desired gloss. (See Illus. 8-4.) You can add additional coats of wax to increase the sheen. Don't expect to get a high gloss; a steel wool–rubbed finish will have a smooth satin gloss.

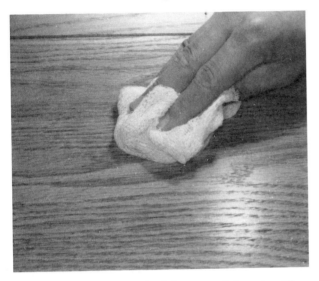

Illus. 8-4. Wipe off most of the wax while it is still a liquid; then let the remaining wax dry, and buff it with a clean, dry cloth.

Wet-or-Dry Sandpaper

Wet-or-dry sandpaper can be used to rub a finish. Use 600- and 1200-grit sandpaper. The 1200-grit sandpaper may be hard to find. You may have to order it from a mail-order woodworking supply company.

After the finish is thoroughly dry, wet-sand the surface with 600-grit sandpaper. Use a flexible rubber sanding block. Dip the sandpaper into a dish of water often to lubricate it and wash off the accumulated residue. (See Illus. 8-5.) Sand in long, straight strokes with the wood's grain. (See Illus. 8-6.) Wipe the surface dry occasionally and check your progress. (See Illus. 8-7.) If there are stubborn shiny spots that can't be removed with the sanding block, make a small pad of sandpaper and move it across the surface with your fingertips. (See Illus. 8-8.)

When the surface is uniformly dull, clean it thoroughly with a damp cloth. Make sure you remove all of the residue. It will contain small pieces of grit from the sandpaper. If this grit is left on the surface during the next step, it can cause scratches.

Illus. 8-5. Wet-or-dry sandpaper can be used to rub the top coat. Use 600-grit sandpaper. Dip the sandpaper in water frequently to keep it clean and wet.

Illus. 8-6. Rub the sandpaper in long, straight strokes with the grain of the wood. Don't make any cross-grain or swirling strokes, because they will become visible in the final surface.

Illus. 8-7. Occasionally wipe the surface dry to check your progress. The surface should be uniform in appearance and free from shiny spots.

Illus. 8-8. Sometimes there are low areas on the surface that will not get rubbed by the sandpaper on the sanding block. Apply finger pressure to a small pad of sandpaper to rub these areas.

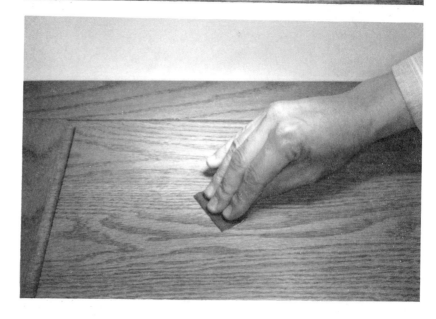

Now, switch to 1200-grit sandpaper. Fold a piece of cheesecloth into a pad about ⅛ inch thick and place it between the sandpaper and the sanding block. This added cushion will help the sandpaper conform to the surface and sand uniformly over the entire area. (See Illus. 8-9.)

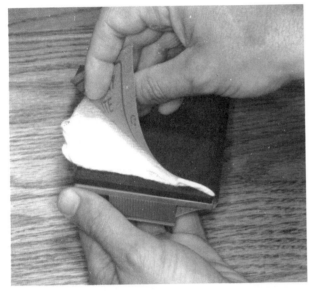

Illus. 8-9. To produce an even finer surface, switch to 1200-grit sandpaper. Fold a piece of cheesecloth into a pad and place it between the sanding block and the sandpaper. This additional cushioning will help the sandpaper conform to surface irregularities and produce an even sheen on the entire surface.

Dip the sandpaper into water, and sand in long, straight strokes with the grain. Dip the sandpaper into the water frequently as you sand. Wipe the surface dry with a clean cloth to examine the surface. When you get a uniform sheen, stop sanding.

Clean and dry the surface, and then apply a coat of wax. Buff the surface until the finish has the desired sheen.

Rubbing Compounds

Rubbing compounds are a blend of lubricants, waxes, and very fine abrasives. (See Illus. 8-10.) There are rubbing compounds available that are

Illus. 8-10. Commercial rubbing compounds are a blend of lubricants, waxes, and abrasives. They usually come in two grades. The finer grade, shown here, is called "polishing compound." The coarser grade is called "rubbing" or "cleaning compound."

made specifically to rub on wood finishes. If you can't find this type, use the type made to rub out automobile finishes. Most auto-parts stores sell this type. It comes in two grades. The finer grade is usually called polishing compound, and the coarser grade is called rubbing or cleaning compound. Both types are useful for wood finishing. The rubbing compound produces a satin finish, and the polishing compound can produce a gloss.

Though a rag can be used to apply the rubbing compound, a felt rubbing block works better. (See Illus. 8-11.) You may have to order the felt rubbing block from a mail-order woodworking supply source.

Begin by wet-sanding the surface with 600-grit sandpaper as described above. (See Illus. 8-12.) Then wipe the surface clean.

The next step is to rub on the rubbing compound. Put some of the rubbing compound on the rag or felt block and wipe it onto the surface in a straight stroke running with the wood's grain. Apply moderate pressure to the pad and rub it back and forth with the grain. (See Illus. 8-13.) Apply more rubbing compound as needed. If the rubbing compound dries out, sprinkle a little water on the surface. If you can't get the felt block into an area like a moulded edge, rub that

Illus. 8-11. A felt rubbing block is a special applicator made specifically for rubbing finishes.

Illus. 8-12. Before rubbing the rubbing compound, wet-sand the surface with 600-grit sandpaper.

Illus. 8-13. Use a felt block or a rag to apply the rubbing compound onto the surface, and rub it in long, straight strokes with the grain.

Illus. 8-14. Use a wad of cheese-cloth to rub the compound in areas such as this raised panel or on moulded edges.

section with a piece of cheesecloth. (See Illus. 8-14.)

Occasionally wipe the surface clean and check your progress. For a higher gloss, repeat the procedure using the finer-grade polishing compound. Use a different rag or felt pad so that there won't be any of the previous abrasive left in the pad.

When you are satisfied with the finish, clean the surface with a wet cloth. Dry the surface; then apply paste wax and buff it to the desired sheen.

Pumice and Rottenstone

The old traditional way to produce a rubbed finish is to use two very fine powdered abrasives called pumice and rottenstone. This method is also the most difficult to master, so the novice should try it only after he has had some experience with the first three methods.

Begin by wet-sanding the surface as described previously. Wipe the surface clean with a wet cloth.

While the surface is still wet, sprinkle some pumice on it. (See Illus. 8-15.) There are several grades of pumice. For this procedure, use the finest grade, called "FFF." Wet a felt pad and rub

it back and forth in long, straight strokes with the grain. (See Illus. 8-16.) Occasionally wipe the surface clean and check your progress. When the surface is uniform, stop. If the satin sheen is satisfactory, stop at this point.

For a higher gloss, remove all of the pumice residue with a wipe cloth and switch to rottenstone. Use a different felt pad. This felt pad should be used only for rottenstone, to ensure that it does not have any pumice on it. Rub the surface using the same procedure that you used

Illus. 8-15. Pumice and rottenstone are dry powders. Wet the surface of the wood, and then sprinkle the powder on.

for the pumice. Stop when the finish has the desired sheen. It is possible to achieve a high degree of gloss when using rottenstone. Finally, apply paste wax and buff it.

Illus. 8-16. Use a wet felt pad to rub the powder. Rub in long, straight strokes with the wood's grain.

Chapter 9
PAINT

When used as a wood finish, paint has two main advantages. First, it makes a durable surface coat. Second, it will hide defects that would appear when a transparent finish is used. Paint is usually selected as a wood finish when the project has to have a certain look. (See Illus. 9-1.)

Illus. 9-1. Paint makes a durable surface coat that will hide defects that would normally appear with a transparent finish. Paint is usually used on furniture and cabinets when a certain look is desired. Many antiques were painted originally. For authenticity, this antique reproduction is being painted in a traditional color.

Paint forms a surface film on top of the wood. This seals out moisture and protects the wood. Only a small amount of the paint soaks into the wood to bond the film to the wood below. Most paint failures can be traced to poor bonding of the paint to the wood.

Surface preparation is just as important when paint is used as it is with other finishes. A surface that has not been properly sanded will show through the paint as a rough surface. Sanding also ensures that the surface will be clean and oil-free. If the surface is oily or dirty, then the paint won't adhere very well.

Choosing Paint

There are several decisions you must make when choosing a paint. First, decide whether to use water- or oil-based paint. Water-based paint is used much more often than oil-based paint for interior and exterior house painting, but for a finer finish on items such as furniture and cabinetry, oil-based paint is more effective. For such work there are two disadvantages to using most of the current semi-gloss or gloss water-based paints. First, they develop a condition called *blocking*, which means that objects left on the painted surface tend to stick to it even after the paint has been dry for a long time. This is not of much concern when it occurs on walls and trim, but it can cause tremendous problems on a bookcase or cupboard. The second problem with water-based paints is that they will raise the grain of wood, leaving a rough surface that must be sanded before the next coat is applied.

So, if a glossy or semi-glossy finish is desired on a piece of furniture or cabinetry, use an oil-based paint. A *flat* water-based paint is perfectly acceptable for furniture or cabinetry when a flat finish is desired. Glossy water-based paints are continually being improved, so it is quite possible that they can also be used in the near future to create a fine finish on furniture or cabinetry.

The next decision you must make concerns the amount of gloss desired. Paint comes in several degrees of gloss, ranging from flat to high. A flat-gloss paint is generally not a good choice for furniture. If a dull surface is desired, use eggshell. Eggshell paint is a satin-gloss paint that looks almost flat, but is smoother and easier to clean than a true flat paint.

Most furniture and cabinetry look best when a semi-gloss paint is used. Such paint creates a glossy finish, but it doesn't reveal fingerprints and small scratches as much as a gloss paint. Use gloss paint when you want a very glossy surface. It is easy to wipe clean, but it will reveal fingerprints and small scratches more than the less glossy paints.

Another decision that has to be made concerns the color of the paint. Color is a choice that depends on personal taste and the style of the piece being painted. One very valuable recent advance in color is the introduction of color-matching computers, which can be found in larger paint outlets. The paint matcher has a scanner that looks at a color sample and then determines the formula for the pigments it will take to match the sample. The color sample can be anything; for example, a small piece of carpet or wallpaper. The color-matching computer can be a big advantage when you are refinishing an old piece and want to duplicate the original shade. In such a situation, find a well-preserved section of the original paint. Clean the area and have paint mixed to match.

The final decision to be made concerns the quality of the paint to be used. For most projects, use the best-quality paint you can find. Large quantities of paint are not needed for furniture and cabinetry, so you can afford to pay more than you would for wall paint. These items must look good, and the paint must be durable.

Applying Paint

Use a good paintbrush to apply paint to furniture and cabinetry. Foam, synthetic-bristle, or natural-bristle brushes can be used. For smooth surfaces, a foam brush works well. If the surface has some texture, then a bristle brush is best.

For a water-based paint, use a brush with synthetic bristles. For an oil-based paint, either a natural- or synthetic-bristle brush can be used. If you are painting a large, flat surface like a tabletop, use a pad applicator.

Painting New Wood

If you are working with wood that hasn't been finished before, begin by sanding the wood as described in Chapter 3. If the wood is open-grained, decide whether or not you want the texture of the wood to show on the painted surface. Open-grained woods such as oak have a prominent pore pattern that will show through several coats of paint. This can be a nice effect. By letting the wood texture show, you retain the character of the wood.

For a completely smooth surface that doesn't show any grain, you can either use a closed-grained wood to build the project, or you can fill the grain of an open-grained wood. To fill grain, use a paste wood filler. Refer to Chapter 3 for directions. Apply the filler after sanding and before applying the primer.

After sanding, use a tack cloth to remove the last remaining dust particles from the project.

It is usually a good idea to apply a primer to bare wood. (See Illus. 9-2.) Follow the manufacturer's recommendation for the type of primer to use. The primer and the top-coat paint must be compatible. Try to use paint and primer from the same manufacturer.

Even if you are planning on using a water-based paint, use an oil-based primer. Water-

Illus. 9-2. Primer should be applied to bare wood. Primer is specifically formulated to adhere to bare wood and prepare it to receive the paint.

based paint can cause the grain to rise on bare wood. This will lead to a rough surface on the finished paint job. By using an oil-based primer, you will seal the wood from moisture before you apply the water-based paint, so that no grain-raising occurs.

Sometimes color from the wood will bleed through paint. This occurs particularly around areas that have knots. If you suspect that this may be a problem on the piece you are painting, use a primer that contains a stain blocker. This will seal the surface so that the stain can't seep through to the top coats. (See Illus. 9-3.)

Let the primer dry, and then rub it with a synthetic finishing pad or sand it with 220-grit sandpaper. (See Illus. 9-4.) Use a tack cloth to remove the sanding dust. Next, apply the first coat of paint. Brush the paint in long, even strokes with the grain direction of the wood. (See Illus. 9-5.) Brush the paint across the surface so that it forms a thin coat. Let the paint dry, and then rub it with a synthetic finishing pad or #000 steel wool. This will remove any dust that got trapped in the wet paint and will also dull the gloss so that the next coat will stick well. A synthetic finishing pad or steel wool works better than sandpaper in this situation, because the

Illus. 9-3. Knots and stains on the wood can bleed through paint. To prevent this, use a stain blocker before applying the paint.

Illus. 9-4. Use a synthetic finishing pad to smooth the paint between coats.

Illus. 9-5. Brush on the paint in long, straight strokes with the grain direction of the wood.

sandpaper will quickly clog up with paint. Next, apply another thin coat. You can stop here or sand the surface again and apply additional coats.

To create a very fine finish on furniture, rub the paint just as you would rub varnish. This will only work with oil-based paint that dries hard. The paint must be thoroughly dry before you rub it. Let the paint dry as long as is practical—usually at least two weeks.

To create a very fine finish on furniture, first rub the surface with #0000 steel wool. When the paint is uniformly dull and smooth, wipe off all of the dust. Then apply rubbing compound. (See Chapter 8.) Use a felt rubbing block or a pad of cheesecloth to rub the surface. (See Illus. 9-6.) If there is an obvious grain direction, rub in long, straight strokes with the grain. If there is no grain visible, you can rub in one direction, or rub in a swirling motion such as would be used when waxing a car. Occasionally sprinkle some water on the surface to keep the rubbing compound wet. Wipe off the residue with a moist cloth. Finally, apply a coat of paste wax and buff the piece with a clean cloth.

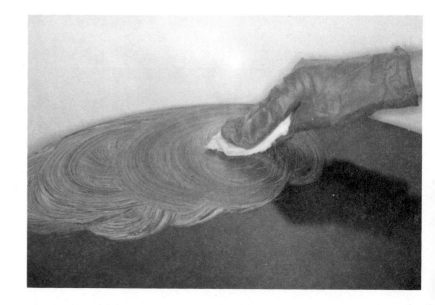

Illus. 9-6. You can rub paint just as you would varnish. This will produce a very smooth satin surface. If there is no discernible grain, use a swirling motion to rub out the paint. If there is a grain visible, rub in straight strokes with the grain.

Painting Particleboard

Particleboard is an inexpensive wood product made from wood chips bonded together into a sheet. When painted correctly, projects made from particleboard can be very attractive. If you have tried to paint particleboard before, you may have been disappointed with the results. Unless you follow the proper procedures, it is likely that the paint finish will turn out rough and unattractive.

Use only oil-based paint on particleboard. Water-based paint will make the surface of the board rough and bumpy. Surface preparation is also very important when particleboard is being painted. There are some high grades of particleboard that have a very smooth surface, but most of the particleboard you will be using has a slightly rough surface. Even sanding will not completely smooth the surface, because of the roughness produced by gaps between the wood particles on the surface. To create a smooth finish, use paste wood filler. The gaps between the particles are about the size of the pores in open-grained wood, so the wood filler will fill them in the same way.

The edges of particleboard are particularly rough. Before proceeding with other finishing steps, fill the rough edges by applying the type of wood putty used to fill nail holes. (See Illus. 9-7.) After the putty is dry, proceed with the sanding.

The surface of particleboard is usually sanded at the factory to the same smoothness as would be achieved by using 100-grit sandpaper, so you can begin sanding with 150-grit sandpaper and then finish with 220-grit. (See Illus. 9-8.) Next, apply the paste wood filler. Thin the filler according to the directions on the can. Brush it on the

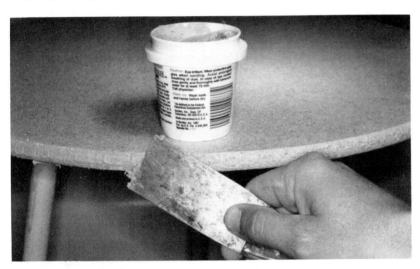

Illus. 9-7. Particleboard edges are very rough and porous. Fill them with wood putty before you paint.

Illus. 9-8. Sand particleboard before you apply paint. A power sander makes the job easy.

surface of the particleboard and let it dry until the gloss is gone. (See Illus. 9-9.)

Now, wipe the excess filler off with a wad of cheesecloth. (See Illus. 9-10.) Let the filler dry overnight. Then rub the surface with a synthetic finishing pad or #000 steel wool. (See Illus. 9-11.) This will remove any filler left on the surface and further smooth the particleboard. Use a vacuum or a brush to remove the sanding dust, and then wipe the surface with a tack cloth before applying the primer.

Next, apply a coat of primer to the particleboard. Use an oil-based primer that is compatible with the top coat you will use. (See Illus. 9-12.) After the primer is dry, rub it with a synthetic finishing pad or sand it with 220-grit sand-paper. (See Illus. 9-13.) As you sand, you will be able to see if the filler has completely filled in the gaps in the surface. If the surface still seems rough after you have sanded the primer, remove all of the sanding dust and apply another coat of primer. This should be enough to completely smooth the surface. Sand this coat with a finishing pad or 220-grit sandpaper. Now you are ready to apply the top coats.

Apply very thin coats of paint. For an extra-smooth finish, use spray paint. (See Illus. 9-14.) If you want to brush on the paint, brush it across the surface very carefully to get a thin, uniform coat. Let the first coat dry completely, and then rub the paint with a synthetic finishing pad or #000 steel wool. Apply several more coats, until

Illus. 9-9. To create a very smooth paint finish on particleboard, apply paste wood filler to the surface before you start to paint.

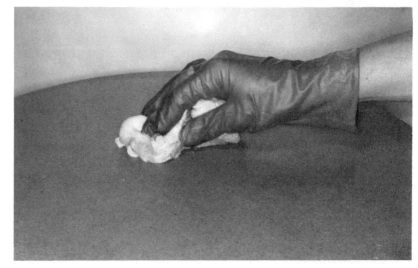

Illus. 9-10. Let the filler dry as specified on the container, and then wipe off the excess with a wad of cheesecloth or burlap.

Illus. 9-11. Let the filler dry overnight, and then rub the surface with a synthetic finishing pad to remove any excess.

Illus. 9-12. Apply a coat of primer to the particleboard. Primer that comes in a spray can is easy to apply.

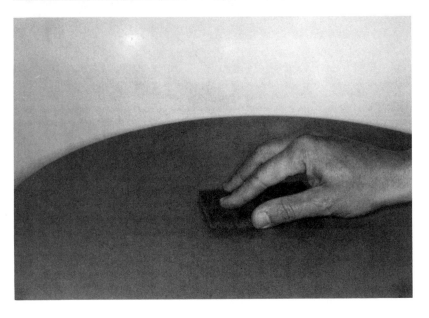

Illus. 9-13. When the primer is dry, rub it with a synthetic finishing pad to smooth the surface. The primer will fill in small pores that weren't filled with the paste wood filler. You can apply a second primer coat if the first coat doesn't look smooth after being rubbed with the finishing pad.

Illus. 9-14. Apply the paint in very thin coats. Using spray paint will eliminate brush marks and produce a professional-looking finish.

you are satisfied with the results. Use a finishing pad or #000 steel wool between each coat, and remove all of the dust with a tack cloth.

Painting Previously Finished Wood

Wood that has been previously finished or painted can be repainted easily, if the old finish is not in terrible condition. If the old finish is cracked or blistered, then remove it. See Chapter 12 for details. If the old finish is sound, then one or two coats of paint are all that are necessary. Primer is not needed, because the old finish has sealed the wood.

The first step is to thoroughly clean the old finish. Use trisodium phosphate (TSP) mixed with water to wash the old finish. TSP is available at most stores that sell paint. It is also an ingredient in some household cleaning products.

Mix the TSP with water in a bucket. Soak a sponge in the solution, and then ring it out and wipe the project's surface with the damp sponge. (See Illus. 9-15.) Make sure that the sponge is damp, not soaked, with water to avoid getting a lot of water on the surface. Frequently rinse the sponge in the bucket of TSP solution. After the surface is clean, dry it with a clean cloth.

The next step consists of dulling the gloss and removing any rough spots. This is done by rubbing the surface with #000 steel wool. You can combine this step with the cleaning step by using a synthetic finishing pad instead of a sponge when you wash the paint with TSP. (See Illus.

9-16.) A special sanding sponge can also be used for this operation. This is a sponge that is coated with abrasives. Use this fine-grit sanding sponge to clean the surface with the TSP solution. Rub the sanding sponge over the surface lightly, and rinse it in the TSP frequently. (See Illus. 9-17.)

Illus. 9-15. When painting over an old finish, first completely clean the surface.

Be careful not to sand too much. Avoid sanding through the finish to bare wood; if you do, you will have to sand and prime the area. Just sand enough to clean and dull the surface of the old finish.

Another way to remove the gloss and clean the surface is to use a chemical deglosser. This is a strong chemical solution that removes grease and some of the surface of the old finish to leave a dull, clean surface for the new paint. These products are strong and can release harmful fumes, so be sure to wear plastic gloves and work in an area with plenty of ventilation.

To use a chemical deglosser, moisten a rag with the deglosser and wipe it on the piece's surface. (See Illus. 9-18.) As the rag becomes covered with dirt and old paint, refold it to expose a clean section and add more deglosser. Rub in one spot

only long enough to remove the gloss. There is no need to remove a lot of the old finish. Then let the deglosser dry as specified on the can before you paint.

Next, repair any dents or gouges with wood putty. Use a putty knife to spread the putty. (See Illus. 9-19.) Leave the putty slightly higher than the surrounding surface. Let the putty dry, and then sand it flush with the surface.

Now, apply the first coat of paint. Brush it on in a thin, uniform coat, and brush across the surface to eliminate drips and overlap marks. (See Illus. 9-20.) If you are using a color that is similar to the original color, you may only need one coat. Usually, two coats will be better. Let the first coat dry, and then rub it with a synthetic finishing pad or #000 steel wool. Wipe the dust off with a tack cloth and apply the second coat.

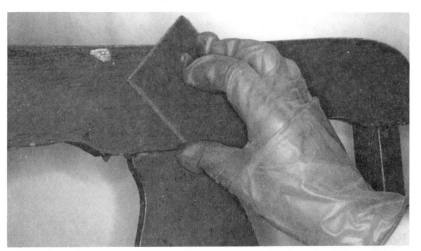

Illus. 9-16. To ensure that the paint will stick to the old finish, rub the surface with the synthetic finishing pad until all of the gloss has been removed.

Illus. 9-17. A sanding sponge is another way to remove the gloss and smooth the surface in preparation for paint.

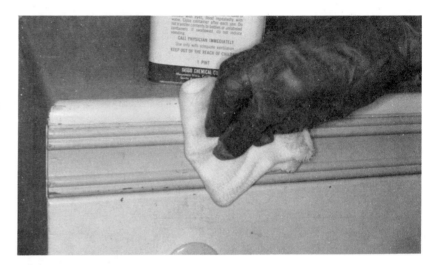

Illus. 9-18. *Deglosser is a chemical that will clean and remove the gloss from the old paint. If the old surface is in good condition, using a deglosser can be an easy way to prepare the project for a new coat of paint.*

Illus. 9-19. *After cleaning and deglossing the old paint, use wood putty to fill any defects in the surface.*

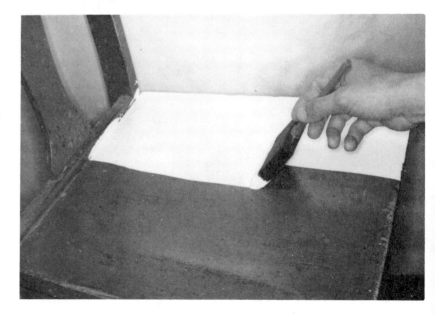

Illus. 9-20. *Now, apply the paint in long, straight strokes with the wood's grain direction. Note that here a foam brush is being used. A foam brush is more effective than a bristle brush because it creates a smoother coat that has fewer brush marks.*

Chapter 10

APPLYING AN ANTIQUE FINISH

When you want to make a new piece of furniture look like an antique, special finishing procedures have to be followed. These begin at the wood-preparation stage and continue through the final top coat. (See Illus. 10-1.)

Illus. 10-1. To make an antique reproduction look like a genuine antique, follow the special finishing procedures described in this chapter.

Wood Preparation

Begin by sanding the wood as you normally would, following the directions in Chapter 3. As you sand, visualize how a real antique would wear. (See Illus. 10-2.) During the first stages of the sanding operation, when you are using the coarse sandpaper, you can simulate the look of a piece of furniture that has become worn through years of use. Normally, you would try to keep the surface flat and preserve sharp corners when sanding, but when an antique look is desired, round off sharp corners and create dips in the surface where extra wear would occur. (See Illus. 10-3.)

A belt sander makes the job of simulating wear easy. Use an 80-grit sanding belt. Begin by sanding the entire surface, and then rounding off the edges. (See Illus. 10-4.) Vary the amount you round an edge, depending on its location. If it is on an area that would receive a lot of day-to-day wear, round it a lot. If it is protected by other parts of the piece, then just round it slightly. Front corners receive a lot of wear; round them heavily.

Next, decide whether to leave all surfaces flat or to simulate wear on them. In the latter situation, decide where the most wear would occur.

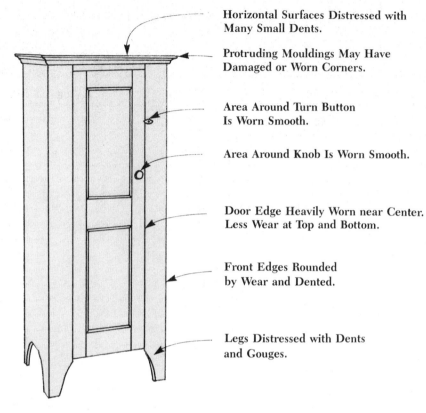

Horizontal Surfaces Distressed with Many Small Dents.

Protruding Mouldings May Have Damaged or Worn Corners.

Area Around Turn Button Is Worn Smooth.

Area Around Knob Is Worn Smooth.

Door Edge Heavily Worn near Center. Less Wear at Top and Bottom.

Front Edges Rounded by Wear and Dented.

Legs Distressed with Dents and Gouges.

Illus. 10-2. Wear occurs at points that are frequently handled or easily damaged. This drawing shows typical wear points on a cupboard.

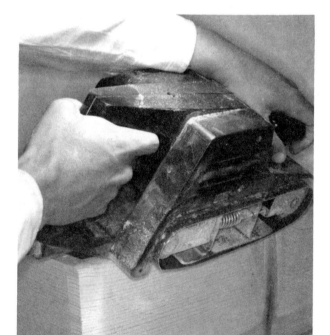

Illus. 10-3. This closeup of a real antique shows how wear has rounded the corners.

Illus. 10-4 (right). Sand the corners and edges to simulate the wear of many years. A belt sander is a good tool for this job.

Then sand a dip in the surface by working the belt sander back and forth over the area.

After the initial sanding, you have to decide whether to make the surface look rough and weathered or smooth and timeworn. This should be determined by your preferences and by the type of project being finished. A rough, weathered look simulates a piece that has been left outside and has not received much care. A smooth, timeworn look simulates one that has been lovingly cared for over many years and burnished to a soft sheen by hundreds of applications of hand-rubbed wax.

To simulate a rough, weathered look, stop sanding after using the 80-grit sandpaper. Now, go over the surface with a wire brush. (See Illus. 10-5.) Though a hand wire brush can be used, for a very weathered look use a wire-brush wheel mounted in an electric drill. (See Illus. 10-6.) Brush with the grain of the wood. The brush will remove the softer parts of the wood, leaving the hard grain pattern standing in relief. The effect

Illus. 10-6. A wire-brush wheel mounted on an electric drill can be used to make the wood look more weathered than is possible with a hand brush.

Illus. 10-5. Wire-brushing wood gives it a weathered look. It removes the softer parts of the grain, leaving the harder parts raised slightly above the surface. This is exactly what happens naturally as wood weathers, so wire-brushed wood looks authentic.

can be varied, depending on the amount of pressure applied to the brush and the length of time spent on each section. Be sure to wear safety glasses or goggles when wire-brushing the wood.

For a smooth, timeworn effect, carefully sand the surface following the directions in Chapter 3. Use a soft-backed sanding block and pay special attention to the edges, rounding-out any marks left by the rough-sanding. Work up to 220-grit sandpaper before staining.

After sanding the entire project with 220-grit sandpaper, go over the edges with finer sandpaper to burnish them and give them a worn look. Burnishing the edges will make them stain slightly lighter than the rest of the wood, heightening the look of natural wear. You can work up to 600-grit sandpaper on the edges, if so desired.

Another way to burnish the edges is to rub them with a smooth stone. (See Illus. 10-7.) A river stone that has been polished and rounded by water works best.

Illus. 10-7. Rubbing the edges with a smooth river stone will burnish them and make them look as if they have become worn naturally.

Distressing

A real antique will have many bumps and gouges. (See Illus. 10-8.) These can be simulated by a process called "distressing." Distressing is simply hitting the surface of the wood with a variety of objects to make dents and gouges in it. Exercise restraint when distressing wood. The result will be a better-looking piece. Keep the marks small and make them at random locations.

Many objects can be used to distress wood. Nuts and bolts, nails, screws, and chains are often used. One distressing tool that is particularly effective is a large steel punch. The one shown in Illus. 10-9 has a round end and a square end. It can make a wide variety of marks, depending on how it hits the wood.

To distress the wood with the large steel punch, first drop the punch on the wood at random. After a while, look at the project to see if there are some areas that need special attention. If some spots seem bare, concentrate the distressing on those areas. (See Illus. 10-10.) Like the procedure used to simulate wear, distressing should be concentrated where it would naturally occur. Working surfaces and edges will get the most marks, while protected areas will get very few.

Next, work over the edges. The edges on a real antique receive many dents and nicks, so give them more marks than the rest of the project. Use the punch again, this time holding it at the

Illus. 10-8. This is a closeup of a genuine antique shelf that has been heavily used. Note the variety of marks on the surface. When you distress a project, you are attempting to simulate this natural distressing that occurs over many years of use. Not all surfaces will show this much distressing. Antiques not as heavily used as this shelf will show less distressing.

Illus. 10-9. This large steel punch makes a very ef-fective distressing tool. Because it has a round end and a square end, it can be used to produce many different kinds of marks, depending on how it strikes the wood.

Illus. 10-11. Edges always get many dents, so hit them with the sides of the punch. The square corners make a V-shaped dent, and the round end makes a rounded dent. Vary the shape, size, and positioning of the dents to give a natural random appearance.

Illus. 10-10. Begin distressing by dropping the punch on the board at random. Then either make additional marks on areas that seem bare or use a different part of the punch to create different-looking marks.

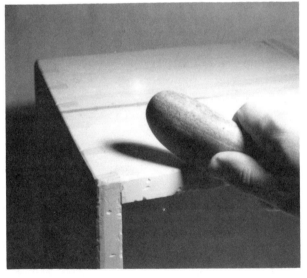

Illus. 10-12. Hit the edges a few times with the river stone to make some large, rounded dents.

round end and hitting the edges with the square corner. (See Illus. 10-11.) Then turn it over and use the round end to make different-looking marks. For large dents, hit the edges in a few locations with the river stone. (See Illus. 10-12.)

Spatter-Distressing

Sometimes the objective is to simulate the look of a distressed piece without actually making dents in the wood. Spatter-distressing is a process in

Illus. 10-13. Spattered paint has been used on this piece to simulate the dents and stains that a real antique would have.

which paint or stain is spattered on the wood to give the piece an antique look. (See Illus. 10-13.)

A 1-inch-wide nylon brush is a good tool to use for spatter-distressing. Dip it in dark stain or in thin, black, or dark brown paint, and then hold it above the surface of the wood. Hold a board below the brush, and then hit the metal ferrule of the brush against the board. (See Illus. 10-14.) This will send a shower of drops down onto the project.

The final effect depends on the size and placement of the drops. Small spots look like fly specks. Larger, irregular splatters look like gouges or dents when viewed from a distance.

Practice on a piece of scrap and you will soon learn how to aim the specks where you want them. Flies like to land on corners and protected areas, so if you are trying to duplicate fly specks, concentrate the specks on those areas. For a more general antique effect, distribute the spatters more evenly all over the surface.

You can apply spatter-distressing before or after applying the top coat. If you spatter-distress after applying the top coat, the spatter will rub off easily, so the spattering is usually added after the stain has been applied and before the shellac or varnish is applied.

Applying the Finish

Although any of the finishes described in this book can be used on an antique reproduction, there are some that will look more authentic than others. A penetrating oil finish is a very good choice for an antique reproduction, because many original pieces were not given much of an original finish, sometimes just a coat of beeswax. The color and sheen seen on antiques today is the result of many years of aging and being rubbed with wax. This is called patina. (See Illus. 10-15.)

A penetrating oil finish in any color can simulate patina. The particular penetrating oil finish

Illus. 10-14. Use a 1-inch-wide nylon brush to make the spatters. Dip it in thin paint or stain, and then hit the metal ferrule against a board that you are holding above the project.

Illus. 10-15. *Patina is the color and sheen on an antique that is the result of many years of wear, rubbing, and waxing. The finish of this reproduction simulates the natural patina of a genuine antique.*

Illus. 10-17. *Sanding in the oil smooths the surface and gives it the look of wood that has been waxed and polished over many years. Note that a darker oil is being used on this oak to simulate the color often found on old oak furniture.*

to be used will be determined by the type of wood you are using. For dark woods like walnut, use a clear oil. For lighter woods like pine, amber or honey-like colors look more authentic than

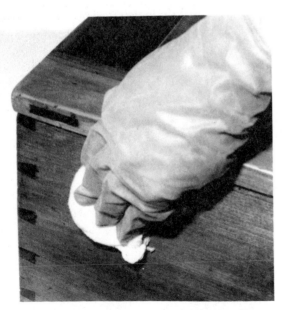

Illus. 10-16. *An amber- or honey-colored oil will imbue pine with the warm glow of genuine patina.*

a very dark shade. (See Illus. 10-16.) If you are trying to create a smooth, timeworn effect, sand in the first coat of oil with 400-grit sandpaper. Sand in the remaining coats with 600-grit sandpaper. (See Illus. 10-17.) For a weathered look, just brush on the oil and let it soak in. (See Illus. 10-18.)

Shellac is an authentic antique finish. Many antiques had shellac applied as the original finish. For the most authentic look, use orange shellac. You can apply it without any stain; this will give the wood the mellow, amber-orange look associated with old wood. But a stain can also be applied first. The orange shellac will darken the stain and give it a mellow look. Follow the directions given in Chapter 5 for applying shellac. (See Illus. 10-19.)

Varnish can also make an antique reproduction look authentic. Apply the desired stain first, and then apply several coats of satin varnish. Buffing the final coat with steel wool gives the finish a soft, timeworn look. (See Illus. 10-20.)

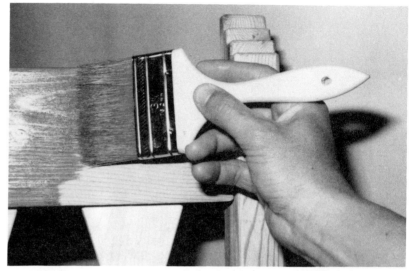

Illus. 10-18. To create a weathered look, brush the oil onto wood that has been wire-brushed. This outdoor bench is being finished with a grey exterior oil finish to make it look as if it has been outside facing the elements for many years.

Illus. 10-19. Orange shellac is an authentic finish that was used on many original pieces. Apply it with a bristle brush.

Illus. 10-20. To give varnish a soft, timeworn look, let it dry completely and then buff it with #0000 steel wool and wax.

Applying Wax

Wax has usually accumulated on the finish of an antique. Your reproduction can be given a more authentic look if you apply wax after the finish has dried. Wax can be applied over any of the finishes described above. Use a dark wax. The wax will build up in the distress marks and other nooks and crannies and will emphasize these fea-tures. Paste wax and liquid wax that have been tinted dark brown are available. Liquid wax that is made especially to be used with penetrating oil finishes is very effective. It has a dark walnut color. (See Illus. 10-21.)

Apply the wax to the surface according to the manufacturer's directions. Let it dry, and then buff it with a clean, dry cloth. (See Illus. 10-22.) Repeat the application several times.

Illus. 10-21. After all other finishing steps are completed and the finish is totally dry, apply several coats of dark wax.

Illus. 10-22. Buff the wax with a soft, dry cloth until the desired luster is achieved.

Chapter 11

PASTEL AND PICKLED FINISHES

Pastel and pickled finishes make wood look as if it has been weathered or has had old paint finish that was worn off or stripped away. (See Illus. 11-1.) White or grey are the most frequently used

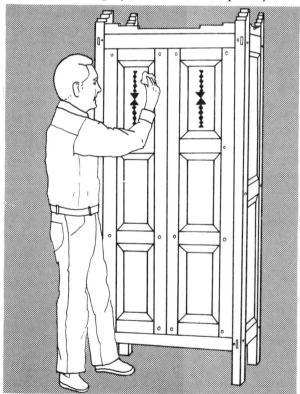

Illus. 11-1. Pastel and pickled finishes can be used on many different styles of furniture. Southwestern-style furniture such as the piece shown here is often given a pickled finish.

colors, but blue, red, green, and other colors can also be used. Pastel and pickled finishes are often applied to antique reproductions, but they can be effective on modern pieces as well. Pickled finishes are often used on small craft projects. Pastel finishes are used a great deal on built-in cabinets. Their light colors make a kitchen bright and cheerful. (See Illus. 11-2.)

Pastel and pickled finishes both require a stain that contains a lot of pigment. The finishes are somewhat similar, but pickled finish is normally rougher and has a more highly accentuated grain pattern. (See Illus. 11-3.) A pastel finish is smoother and has a more subtle grain pattern. Also, a pastel finish has mostly white pigment. The white can be used alone, or small amounts of additional color can be added. A pickled finish looks more like paint that has been stripped or weathered off. It may have white pigments, but other intense colors, such as blue, green, or red, can also be used. Intense colors can be effective for highlighting details on a project such as a carving. (See Illus. 11-4.)

Several products can be used for pastel or pickled finishes. You can buy ready-made pastel stain or make your own from paint. The easiest method is to use pastel rubbing oil. Unlike the normal type of stain used with rubbing oil—a dye stain—pastel stains contain a large amount of white pigment and small amounts of dye or other color pigments. The pigments accumulate

Illus. 11-2. Pastel finishes are well suited to modern furniture and cabinetry. Their light colors give a kitchen a bright, cheerful look.

Illus. 11-3 (left). A pickled finish gives the project a rustic look. It is rougher and has a more highly accentuated grain pattern than a pastel finish. Illus. 11-4 (above). Intense colors like red, blue, and green are being used to highlight the details on this carving. Note that even with these deep colors, the grain still shows through. This is a characteristic of a pickled finish.

in the pores of the wood and highlight the grain pattern.

Pastel finishes have different effects on different types of wood. If you use them on a ring-porous wood such as oak, the pigments will accentuate the pore pattern. (See Illus. 11-5.) When you use them on closed-grained woods such as birch, there is more control over the final effect, because you can vary the intensity of the color by how hard you rub the stain. (See Illus. 11-6.)

Pastel finishes are also very effective on soft-woods like pine; in this case, the pigments accumulate in the softer parts of the grain. (See Illus. 11-7.) When you apply a pastel stain to a diffuse-porous open-grained wood such as Philippine mahogany, the stain color will be more intense and the grain will be less noticeable, because the pigments will accumulate in the evenly distributed pores. (See Illus. 11-8.)

Illus. 11-5. A pastel finish applied to a ring-porous wood such as oak will accentuate the pore pattern.

Illus. 11-6. The effect a pastel stain has on closed-grained woods such as birch is more subtle. The grain pattern is visible beneath a uniform layer of pigment. The amount of pigment left on the surface can be controlled by how hard you rub when you wipe off the stain.

Illus. 11-7. Pastel stains have a nice effect on softwoods such as pine, as shown here. The pigments will accumulate more in the softer portions of the grain, highlighting the grain pattern.

Illus. 11-8. Diffuse-porous, open-grained woods such as this Philippine mahogany will absorb more stain because of the evenly distributed open pores. This will make the color look more intense.

Surface Preparation

Unlike other oil finishes, pastel finishes are used more effectively when the surface of the board has been roughened somewhat. This texture gives the pigments a place to accumulate. To prepare the wood, sand it as described in Chapter 3, but stop with 150-grit sandpaper. For a pickled finish, go over the surface of the wood with a wire brush. This will accentuate the pores. For a slight accentuation, wire-brush lightly with the wood's grain. (See Illus. 11-9.) You can vary the effect by how long and hard you brush.

Pastel Penetrating Oil

When the surface has been prepared, apply the pastel penetrating oil. If the oil is a liquid, apply it with a brush, to create a heavy coat. If it is a gel, use a rag to apply it. (See Illus. 11-10.) Let the oil soak into the wood for a few minutes, and then wipe the surface with a clean cloth.

You can vary the color intensity by wiping hard to remove more pigment or wiping lightly to leave most of the pigment on the board. To create an antique effect, wipe most of the pigment off

Illus. 11-9. To prepare the wood for a pickled finish, lightly wire-brush the surface to open up the pores.

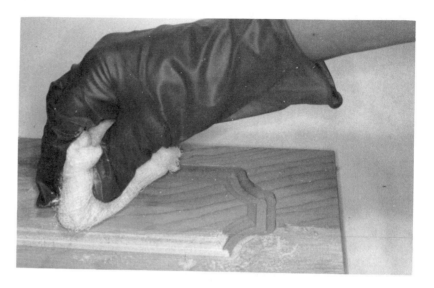

Illus. 11-10. A pastel penetrating oil finish can be wiped on with a rag.

the corners and areas that would likely get a lot of wear. Leave more of the pigment in areas that would not receive much wear.

A pastel finish can be used to highlight carvings and other details. Wipe most of the finish off the flat areas, and leave a buildup of finish in the deep parts of the details. (See Illus. 11-11.) To increase the contrast, apply a standard oil finish first, and apply the pastel oil as a second coat. This will enable you to rub most of the pastel finish off some areas, leaving the standard oil finish visible. (See Illus. 11-12.)

Usually one coat is enough, but if you want a finish with more color, add another coat. This is a stand-alone finish, so there is no need to add anything else.

Pastel Stain

The procedure for applying pastel stain is very similar to the procedure for rubbing oil. The main difference is that a pastel stain is not a finish that can stand by itself, so a top coat has to be applied after the stain has dried. Test the stain on a scrap of the same type of wood as that of your project. If too much stain is absorbed by the wood, making it difficult to wipe the stain to the desired effect, apply a coat of wood conditioner to the surface before applying the stain. Apply the stain with a brush. In this case, use a bristle brush because, unlike a foam brush, it can be used to work the stain into the pores. (See Illus. 11-13.)

Illus. 11-11. A pastel finish can be used to highlight carvings and other details. When you wipe the finish off, leave more finish in the recesses and less on the flat surfaces.

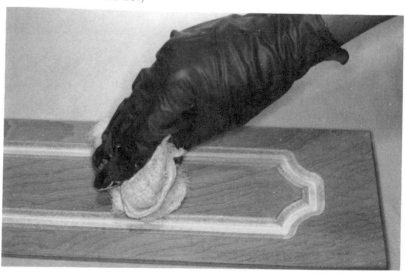

Illus. 11-12 (left). A nice effect can be created by applying a standard penetrating oil as the first coat, and then using a pastel oil finish as the second coat. When you wipe off the second coat, most of the color of the first coat will show through, but the pastel pigments will accumulate in the details. Illus. 11-13 (above). Apply pastel stain with a bristle brush, so that you can work it into the pores of the wood.

Since wiping is crucial to the process, apply the stain to small areas and wipe them before moving to the next section. (See Illus. 11-14.) If you let the stain dry too long, you won't be able to wipe it off, and the finish will look more like paint than stain. If you are having trouble wiping the stain off, moisten a cloth with a compatible thinner and then wipe.

After the stain has dried completely, rub the surface with a synthetic finishing pad to smooth it and remove additional pigment, if necessary. (See Illus. 11-15.) Next, apply the varnish. A high gloss is usually not desired with this type of finish, so choose a satin-gloss varnish. Don't use a varnish that has an amber color, or the finish will have a yellowed look. Use a varnish that dries

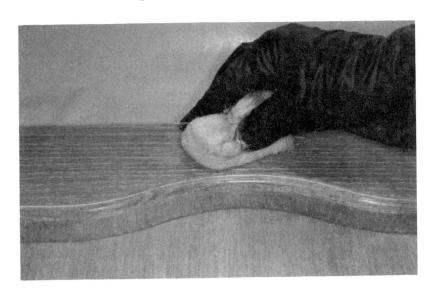

Illus. 11-14. Wipe off the stain before it has a chance to dry. If it sits on the wood for too long, the color may be more intense than desired.

Illus. 11-15. After the stain is dry, rub it smooth with a synthetic finishing pad.

completely clear. Make sure that the varnish is compatible with the stain. Some water-based varnishes are not recommended for use over pastel stains, so be sure to read the label. If the wood is rough, use a bristle brush to apply the varnish; otherwise, a foam brush works better. (See Illus. 11-16.) Refer to Chapter 6 for details on applying varnish.

Pickling with Paint

Ordinary paint can be used to create a pickled finish. Either latex or oil-based paint can be used. Oil-based paint makes a nicer finish, but it is more difficult to clean up. Latex paint dries quickly, so work quickly. In most cases, use white paint, unless a very intense color is desired.

Begin by thinning the paint. Add one part thinner to three parts paint. Use water to thin latex paint. Use paint thinner to thin oil-based paint. (See Illus. 11-17.) If you want a color other than white, start with thinned white paint, and then add a small amount of tinting color. (See Illus. 11-18.) Use it sparingly. Mix thoroughly, and you are ready to begin applying the paint.

Brush the paint onto one section of the project. Work on one small area at a time. (See Illus. 11-19.) Immediately wipe the paint off with a rag. (See Illus. 11-20.) Add thinner to the rag, if necessary, to remove enough of the paint to let the grain of the wood show through.

Let the paint dry overnight, and then rub the surface with a synthetic finishing pad to remove

Illus. 11-16. Apply a top coat of varnish to protect the stain. Use a water-based varnish, if it is compatible with the stain being used. Some manufacturers recommend that you don't use their water-based varnish over an oil-based pastel stain.

Illus. 11-17. Paint can be used as a pickling stain. Thin the paint by adding one part thinner to three parts paint. Use the type of thinner recommended on the paint can.

Illus. 11-18. Some color can be added to the white paint with tinting colors. Use tinting colors that are compatible with the paint being used.

Illus. 11-19. Brush the thinned paint onto a small section of the project.

Illus. 11-20. Wipe the paint off immediately with a rag, before it has a chance to dry.

any raised grain and smooth out any other rough-ness. (See Illus. 11-21.) If you decide that more paint needs to be removed from the surface, rub hard with the finishing pad until you are satisfied with the result.

Finally, apply two coats of clear satin varnish. Make sure that the varnish is compatible with the paint used. Some water-based products won't adhere well to paint, so read the instructions carefully before buying the varnish. If the directions state that the product can be applied over paint, then it is suitable for this application.

Illus. 11-21. After the paint is dry, rub the surface with a synthetic finishing pad. This will smooth out any rough areas and help to even out the color.

Chapter 12
REFINISHING

Removing layers of old paint to reveal the natural beauty of the wood below can be a very satisfying experience. (See Illus. 12-1.) There are still nice old pieces of furniture available at bargain prices that simply need to be refinished to be transformed into the centerpiece of a room.

Before beginning a finishing project, be aware of two very important points. First, if you suspect that the piece you have is a valuable antique, *don't* refinish it. Removing the original finish can decrease the value of an antique. Talk to someone knowledgeable about antiques, if you are in doubt. Second, if you suspect that the piece has been painted with lead paint, don't strip it yourself. Lead paint is potentially very dangerous. The stripping process frees the lead, which can cause severe health problems. This is particularly dangerous for children and pregnant women.

You can buy a testing kit that will indicate whether the paint contains lead. One type of test kit contains chemically treated swabs. If the swabs change color when they are wiped over the paint, then the paint contains high levels of lead. (See Illus. 12-2.) You can also take a sample to your local health department for testing.

If the old paint contains lead, take the project to a professional stripper to have it removed. Professional strippers have the equipment and knowledge to handle the lead.

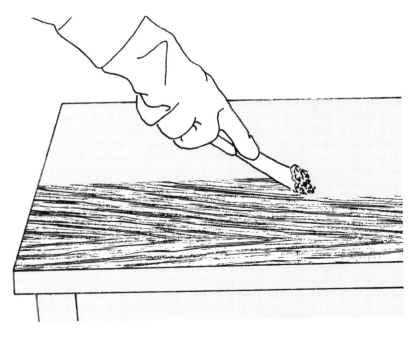

Illus. 12-1. Although there is a lot of work involved, it is very satisfying when you can reveal the natural beauty of a piece of wood that has been hidden under coats of old paint.

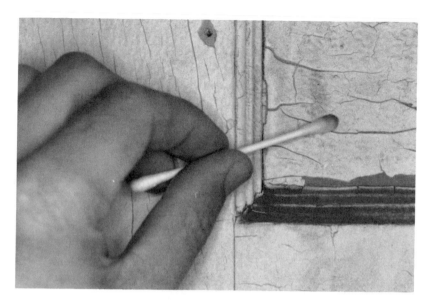

Illus. 12-2. Stripping lead paint can be hazardous. You can use a test kit to determine if the wood has lead paint. This type of test kit uses a chemical on a cotton swab. If the color of the swab changes when it is applied to the paint, then high concentrations of lead are present. You can also send a sample of the paint to a lab for analysis. If it turns out that your project has lead paint, have a professional stripping company remove the paint, and then apply the new finish.

As wood ages, it develops a mellow color and sheen called patina. The patina develops only on a thin layer of the wood's surface. When refinishing an old piece, try to preserve as much of the patina as possible.

An old finish can be removed by using either a refinisher or a stripper. A refinisher is used when the piece has not been painted. It gently removes the old top coats and preserves the original color and sheen of the wood. A stripper is needed when the piece has been painted. A stripper is more likely to raise the grain and cause some damage to the wood. This means that you will have to sand the wood after using stripper. If heavy sanding is required, some of the patina will be lost.

Using a Refinisher

A refinisher will remove old varnish or shellac. It may not work with some modern synthetic finishes. Refinisher is a thin liquid. It may emit harmful fumes, so read the instructions and follow them carefully. Work outside, if possible. Wear plastic gloves. Use goggles to prevent the refinisher from splashing into your eyes. If the area you are working in does not have good ventilation, wear a respirator that is designed to filter out harmful vapors.

Fill a small pan with the refinisher. (See Illus. 12-3.) Dip a steel-wool pad into the refinisher. Use extra-fine steel wool (#0000). Rub the pad in

Illus. 12-3. When using a refinisher, frequently dip a pad of steel wool into the liquid and remove the accumulating finish. Pour the refinisher into a shallow pan or dish to make it more convenient to clean the pad.

a circular motion over a small area about 12 inches in diameter. (See Illus. 12-4.) As the pad loosens the finish, it will fill up with particles of the old finishing material. Dip the pad into the pan of refinisher to remove the residue, and then continue rubbing. When the old top coat has been removed, stop. You don't want to remove the underlying stain and filler, if it is possible to save them.

Illus. 12-4. Rub the steel-wool pad soaked with refinisher in a circular motion over a small area of the project. Keep rubbing until the old top coat has been removed, but stop before you damage the underlying stain and natural patina. As the pad becomes clogged with old finish, dip it into clean refinisher to wash out the residue.

Now, move to the next section. When you have removed all of the old top coat from an area such as a door or tabletop, put fresh refinisher on a clean pad of steel wool and wipe across the entire surface with the grain of the wood. (See Illus. 12-5.) Wipe the surface clean with a piece of cheesecloth moistened with refinisher. (See Illus. 12-6.) Let the surface dry until all of the refinisher has evaporated and you are ready to apply the new finish. No additional sanding is required.

Using Stripper

When the old finish is paint, stripper has to be used. Do not use strippers that contain methylene chloride. This chemical has been shown to be hazardous. There are several new types of strippers available that use less hazardous materials. They are effective, but they may have to be left on the surface longer to soften the old paint.

Follow the directions on the stripper carefully. Even though these new strippers are safer than those that use methylene chloride, still wear plastic gloves and goggles. Use caution when using stripper on plywood or veneered surfaces. If you leave the stripper on too long, the glue that attaches the veneer can become loose.

Most of the new safer strippers consist of a thick liquid that will cling to the surface. (See Illus. 12-7.) Apply a heavy coat of stripper with a

Illus. 12-5. After you have removed the top coat from a section of the project, use a clean steel-wool pad and fresh refinisher to wipe off any remaining residue. Wipe the pad in long, straight strokes with the wood's grain.

Illus. 12-6. Give the wood a final cleaning by wiping it with a clean cloth that is moistened with refinisher.

Illus. 12-7. Modern strippers are safer than the older ones that contain methylene chloride. They are, for the most part, thick liquids that will cling to any surface.

When the old paint has softened, use a putty knife to scrap the residue from the surface. (See Illus. 12-10.) Always scrape the paint off with the grain direction. Scraping across the grain can leave gouges that are hard to remove.

In areas where a putty knife can't be used, rub the residue off with a stripping pad. This is a plastic material that works like steel wool. (See Illus. 12-11.) Don't use steel wool, because it can react with the stripper and leave dark stains on the wood. Rub the pad in straight strokes with the wood's grain direction. (See Illus. 12-12.) The stripping pad is very coarse and can leave deep scratches if it is rubbed across the wood's grain.

brush. (See Illus. 12-8.) Let the stripper remain on the project until the old finish is thoroughly softened. You may need to leave it on overnight to soften a thick coat of paint. To increase the effectiveness of the stripper, cover the project with a disposable plastic tarp after applying the stripper. (See Illus. 12-9.) This slows down the evaporation of the stripper so that it will remain active longer.

Illus. 12-8. Apply a heavy coat of stripper with a brush.

Illus. 12-9. If the paint is thick, you may have to leave the stripper on the project overnight. Cover the project with a disposable plastic tarp to help slow down the evaporation of the stripper.

Illus. 12-10. When the paint is soft, use a putty knife to scrape it off. Always scrape with the grain to avoid cross-grain scratches that can be difficult to remove.

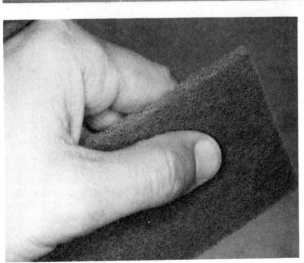

Illus. 12-11. Steel wool will react to the new water-based strippers, so use only synthetic stripping pads. The stripping pads come in three grades; use the coarsest one for stubborn spots. The next grade is used for most work, and the finest grade is used to remove the remaining residue after most of the paint has been removed.

Illus. 12-12. *Rub the stripping pad over the work with the wood's grain direction. Rubbing it across the wood's grain can result in visible scratches.*

Illus. 12-14. *Now, dampen with fresh stripper a stripping pad that is one grade finer than the previous one, and wipe the entire surface.*

This flexible pad can be used to remove most of the paint from mouldings. To get the last remaining areas in small details like mouldings and shaped edges, use a piece of wood dowel, sharpened to a point. (See Illus. 12-13.)

After most of the old finish is removed, dampen a finer stripping pad with some fresh stripper and wipe the entire surface. (See Illus. 12-14.) Next, scrub the surface with a clean, synthetic finishing pad dampened with water. (See Illus. 12-15.) A finishing pad is finer than a stripping pad. It will help to smooth out any rough-

ness left by the stripping pad and remove any raised grain. Finally, wipe the surface dry with a dry cloth. (See Illus. 12-16.)

The stripper will raise the grain of the wood. Rubbing with the finishing pad will usually remove the raised grain, but if the surface still seems rough, sand the wood before applying a

Illus. 12-13. *Use a wood dowel sharpened like a pencil to remove the paint residue from mouldings and details.*

Illus. 12-15. *Use a fine finishing pad to smooth the wood and remove the last of the paint residue. The finishing pads are effective for getting into tight places such as the details of this turned chair leg.*

Illus. 12-16. Wipe off any remaining stripper with a dry cloth.

finish. (See Illus. 12-17.) Lightly sand the surface with 320-grit sandpaper. As soon as you remove the raised grain fibres, stop sanding. You don't want to sand too deep; you want to preserve as much of the patina as possible. Let the wood dry overnight. When it is dry, it is time to apply a finish.

Illus. 12-17. If there is any remaining roughness on the wood, sand it with 320-grit sandpaper. Don't sand any more than necessary, because sanding can remove the natural patina.

Applying the Finish

If you were able to preserve the patina of the wood, you may only want to apply a clear top coat. If you want to change the color, or if the wood looks blotchy, stain the wood first. If there are dark stains on the wood, these can sometimes be removed with a chemical bleach. Use the type specifically made for bleaching wood, and follow the directions and safety precautions on the container. It is best to bleach the entire surface to get a uniform color. When bleaching a vertical surface, start at the bottom and work up. That way bleach that drips down won't cause streaks in the wood below. If you bleach out a stain, it will lighten the underlying wood also, so you will have to stain the project if you want a darker color.

A rubbed oil finish makes a good top coat when a refinisher has been used. Apply several coats of the finish, following the directions in Chapter 4. (See Illus. 12-18.) The refinisher will usually leave the wood with a nice color and surface, so a clear oil finish will work well. If you want to darken the color of the wood, use an oil finish-stain.

Any of the other top coats described in this book can be applied to a project that has been treated with refinisher, but test them on an inconspicuous spot first, in case the old finishing material in the wood and the new finish are incompatible. Orange shellac will give the project an authentic antique look. Varnish is more durable than shellac and will work better for projects that will receive a lot of use.

Projects that have been stripped will usually take more work to refinish. The stripping process removes more of the original finish and can leave a rough surface. The process involved in such a case is similar to that used when starting with new wood. If the stripped wood has a nice color and patina, try to preserve it. A clear oil finish will enhance the natural color of the wood and protect it. In many cases, it is necessary to apply a stain to even out the color of the wood.

After you have applied a stain, you can apply varnish, shellac, or lacquer.

Varnish can be applied over a stripped surface.

Refer to Chapter 6 for details. Shellac is an authentic antique finish.

Illus. 12-18. Let the project dry for several days, and then apply a new finish. If you were able to preserve the color and patina of the wood, all that is needed to do is to apply a clear oil finish.

GLOSSARY

Abrasives Products used to smooth the wood before the finish is applied.

Backing The material that abrasive particles are attached to in coated abrasives. Paper, cloth, and fibreboard are common backings.

Belt Sander A power tool that has a continuous abrasive belt stretched between two rollers, and that is used for initial sanding.

Blocking A condition in which the finish clings to objects placed upon it.

Cambium A layer of cells just beneath the bark of a tree, where new growth occurs.

Chemical Deglosser A strong chemical solution used to remove the gloss and clean the surface of an old finish.

Closed-Coat Sandpaper Sandpaper that has the entire surface of the backing covered with abrasive particles. It cuts fast but clogs easily.

Cloth-backed Abrasive Abrasive in which the grit is attached to heavy cloth.

Cut The relationship between the weight of dry flakes and the volume of solvent used in making shellac. A one-pound cut consists of one pound of dry shellac flakes dissolved in one gallon of solvent.

Danish Oil A penetrating oil finish made from a mixture of oils, driers, resins, and solvents. It is generally easier to use than pure tung oil.

Diffuse-Pore Wood Wood with pores that are evenly distributed throughout its ring.

Distressing The process of intentionally damaging a finish to give it an antique look.

Dye A coloring agent used in stains that soaks into the wood. Dyes dissolve in the liquid vehicle of the stain and do not "settle out" like pigments.

Filler A product used to fill up the pores of open-grained wood.

Fisheyes Small, round depressions in a finished surface. They are frequently caused when the surface is contaminated with silicones.

Foam Brush A brush that substitutes a single piece of sponge-like plastic foam for the individual filaments of a standard brush.

French Polishing The process of applying shellac with a pad in a series of steps.

Glazing, or Shading A process used to apply colored lacquer in which a thin, even coat is applied to the entire surface, and then more lacquer is applied around the edges and on details.

Gloss Finishes designated as gloss or high gloss dry to a smooth, shiny surface. The opposite of gloss is flat.

Grain The pattern produced by the annual rings in a piece of wood. Grain also refers to the direction of the wood fibres. For example, "sanding with the grain" means moving the sandpaper in strokes that parallel the length of the wood fibres.

Grain-Raising A condition that occurs on the surface of a board when its wood fibres absorb water, which causes them to stand up. This produces a rough texture in the finish.

Grit Abrasive particles used in coated abrasives. The term is often used when referring to the grade (coarseness) of an abrasive.

Hardwood Wood derived from broad-leafed trees. The term has no relation to the actual hardness of the wood. *See* Softwood.

Heartwood   Wood from the center portion of the log. It is generally darker and more decay-resistant than the younger sapwood.

Knot   The intersection between a limb and the trunk of a tree that shows up in sawed lumber as a round, oval, or spike-shaped area that is darker and harder than the surrounding wood. A "tight" knot is firmly attached to the surrounding wood. A "loose" knot has a layer of bark between it and the surrounding wood and may eventually fall out, leaving a hole in the board. The grain pattern changes sharply around a knot, making it difficult to plane out.

Lacquer   A tough, fast-drying finish that contains very strong solvents. The solvents in lacquer will dissolve most other finishes. For this reason, lacquer should not be applied directly on top of an old finish other than lacquer. It is usually applied by spraying, but brushing lacquers are available.

Open-Coat Sandpaper   Sandpaper that has empty space surrounding each abrasive particle, as opposed to closed-coat, which has the backing surface completely covered with grit. It doesn't cut as fast as closed-coat initially, but it will last longer when used on materials that tend to clog up the sandpaper.

Pad Applicator   A finishing tool that consists of a foam pad covered with a piece of short-napped fabric that is well suited for applications such as applying stain.

Particleboard   A man-made reconstituted wood product. It is made from very small wood chips or particles bonded together with glue under heat and pressure.

Pastel Finish   A finish that contains a lot of white pigment, along with other colors. When applied to wood, it gives a weathered or worn look. Pastel finishes are often applied to antique reproductions.

Paste Wood Filler   A product specifically designed to fill the small pores on the wood's surface.

Patina   The condition of wood and its finish that develops over time. Usually it is characterized by a smooth, worn surface and darkening of the wood. Also it includes the buildup of waxes and oils that have been applied to wood over time as well as the scars and marks that are acquired through use.

Penetrating Finishes   Thin-bodied finishes that soak into the wood.

Pickled Finish   A finish applied to wood that gives it a weathered or worn look. Pickled finishes are often applied to antique reproductions.

Pigment   A coloring agent used in stains that forms a thin layer on top of the wood. Pigments are made from chemical or natural minerals and ground to very fine particles. They do not dissolve in the liquid vehicle of the stain, so they tend to settle to the bottom of the can and must be thoroughly mixed before use.

Pith   A small, dark growth pattern located in the center of a log.

Plain-sawn Lumber   Wood that has been cut so that the annual rings make an angle of less than 45 degrees with the surface of the board. Also called flat-grained or plain-sawn.

Plywood   A sheet material made by gluing thin layers of wood together with the grain direction of each layer running at right angles to the next one.

Polyurethane   A widely used synthetic resin varnish that produces a very durable finish that is resistant to wear and abrasion, water, and weathering. It is very resistant to chemicals and retains its gloss longer than most finishes under hard wear.

Pores   Small openings in the surface of a board. They result when the saw cuts open large, elongated cells (vessels) in the wood. The vessels serve as fluid channels in the living tree.

Pumice   A light volcanic glass that, in powdered form, is used for rubbing a finish. It is coarser than rottenstone.

Putty   A pasty compound used to fill nail holes and defects in wood.

Quarter-sawn Lumber   Wood that has been cut so that the annual rings form an angle of 45 to 90 degrees with the surface. Also called edge-grained, or vertical-grained.

Rays   Grain features that appear as small, dark lines on the face of plain-sawn lumber. In quarter-sawn lumber, rays appear as prominent irregular grain markings.

Refinisher A product that dissolves the old top coat of varnish or shellac. When it is used carefully, the underlying stain and filler can be preserved.

Refinishing Removing layers of old paint to reveal the natural beauty of the wood.

Resin A synthetic or natural chemical that dries to a hard, impervious film.

Ring-porous Wood Wood with pores that are concentrated in its spring wood.

Rottenstone A natural abrasive made from powdered limestone. It is finer than pumice and is often used for a final rubbing of a finished surface.

Rubbed Finish A silky-smooth finish that is usually applied to a flat surface. The top coat of a rubbed finish is rubbed with fine abrasives to smooth the surface.

Rubbing Compound A commercially prepared mixture of abrasive powder and lubricant that is used for a final rubbing of a finished surface.

Rubbing Varnish A varnish made with natural resins and oils that is formulated to dry hard and be rubbed well with abrasives.

Runs Defects that occur when too much finishing material is applied to a vertical surface.

Sandpaper A coated abrasive with a paper backing. Originally the term applied only to flint paper, but now is applied to any type of abrasive paper.

Sapwood The *live* wood near the outside of a tree. It is generally lighter in color and more prone to decay than heartwood, which is in the center of a log.

Satin A term used to describe a finish that is not as dull as a flat finish, but does not have a high gloss.

Shading Lacquer A lacquer that contains dyes or pigments to color it. It is a semi-transparent surface coating that does not penetrate into the wood. It is used extensively on mass-produced furniture.

Shellac A finishing material made from natural resin that is most commonly used to refinish antiques and to finish antique reproductions.

Silicon Carbide One of the hardest synthetic abrasives used for wood finishing. Its most common use in wood finishing is in wet-or-dry sandpaper.

Softwood Wood produced by trees that have needles rather than broad leaves. The term has no relation to the actual hardness of the wood.

Solvent A liquid used to dissolve other substances.

Spatter-distressing A process in which paint or stain is spattered on the wood to give the piece an antique look.

Stain Any of several products used to artificially color wood. Stains may have dyes, pigments, or chemicals that produce the color. Stains may either penetrate into the wood, form a film on the surface, or react chemically with substances in the wood.

Steel Wool An abrasive material composed of long, fine steel shavings that is used to smooth wood and finish layers. It should not be used with water-based finishes because the steel particles left on the wood can react with water to cause a dark spot.

Stripper Any product that uses chemicals or solvents to soften an old finish for removal.

Stripping Pad A plastic material used to remove residue from the surface of wood.

Surface Finishes Heavy-bodied finishes that form a thin film on top of the wood's surface.

Synthetic Finishing Pad A plastic substitute for steel wool. It lasts longer than steel wool, and can be used with water-based finishes.

Tack Cloth A piece of cheesecloth that has been treated so that it attracts dust.

Tinting Colors Pigments suspended in any of several liquids. They are used to tint or color finishing products.

Tipping-off The final step in applying a varnish in which the brush is held straight up and down so that just the tip touches the surface.

TSP (Trisodium Phosphate) A product that when mixed with water can be used to clean an old finish.

Oil   A natural oil derived from the seeds of the Chinese tung tree. It is used by itself or mixed with other oils to make penetrating oil finishes. It is also used in many paints and varnishes. It dries faster and harder than linseed oil. Also called China wood oil, China nut oil, or nut oil.

Varnish   A transparent finish made with natural or synthetic resins and oils. A varnish hardens by combining with oxygen and is more resistant to water and alcohol than shellac.

Varnish Stain   A colored varnish that stains and varnishes the surface in one step.

Vehicle   The liquid part of a stain. It consists of the solvents, oils, and resins.

Wet-or-dry Sandpaper   Sandpaper that uses waterproof glue to attach the abrasive particles to a water-resistant paper backing.

Wood Conditioner   A sealer used on wood that makes it absorb a stain evenly.

Wood Putty   A doughy product used to fill nail holes and defects in wood.

Wrinkles   Finishing defects that occur when the underlying finish dries more slowly than the top surface. This causes the top surface to have a wrinkled texture.

Index

Basics Series

Band Saw Basics
Cabinetry Basics
Finishing Basics
Joinery Basics
Radial Arm Saw Basics
Router Basics
Scroll Saw Basics
Sharpening Basics
Table Saw Basics

Other Books by Sam Allen

Cabinetry Basics
Joinery Basics
Making Cabinets & Built-Ins
Making Kitchen Cabinet Accessories
Remodelling & Repairing Kitchen Cabinets
Wood Finisher's Handbook
Wood Joiner's Handbook